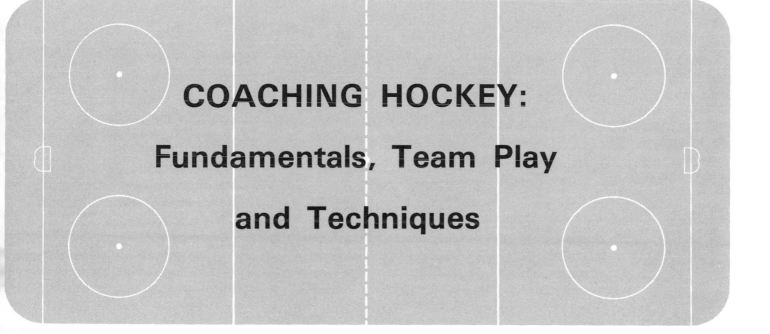

COACHING HOCKEY:

Fundamentals, Team Play

and Techniques

JOHN W. MEAGHER

COACHING HOCKEY:

Fundamentals, Team Play

and Techniques

PRENTICE-HALL, INC.

Englewood Cliffs, N.J.

Library of Congress Catalog No. 72-506
ISBN 0-13-139188-7

Printed in the United States of America

This manual is respectfully dedicated to

all boys who play hockey for fun,

their coaches who provide the essential leadership

and to those fathers who drive their sons to the arena

-and stay to watch them play.

Contents

Preface

This book has been prepared to meet the expressed needs of beginning *and* experienced coaches. For many years hockey coaches have been looking for a text that contains information, data and suggestions that can be applied in situations involving players from pee-wee to professional.

Excellent hockey performance results from a mastery of the fundamental skills of skating, puck-handling, passing, shooting and checking. This text provides the coach with lists of cues and game-like drills that might be used in focusing the attention of the players on fundamental skill learning and improvement.

But, because hockey is a team sport, considerable attention has been given to the application of these fundamental skills in team offensive and defensive situations. Offensive patterns are presented beginning with the process of bringing the puck out of the defensive zone, then through the neutral zone, into the attacking zone, and finally into scoring situations. Defensive patterns are presented beginning with one-man and two-man forechecking systems in the attacking zone, and proceeding to backchecking systems and man-for-man and zone responsibilities in the defensive zone.

Because the goaltender is the single most important defensive player on a team and because he merits and requires the greatest amount of individual coaching attention, a special section has been devoted to his responsibilities, his training and his skill development.

Mastery of the fundamental skills and of offensive and defensive patterns can best be achieved when the players are properly conditioned to learn without undue and restricting fatigue, and when the coach is able to communicate, analyze, correct and direct his players in a manner consistent with the best principles of teaching and learning. Thus, the teaching/coaching process is considered in some detail and, in addition, specific suggestions for player conditioning are provided for use in the off-season, pre-season, early-season, and mid-season periods.

Finally, the text attempts to provide answers to fifteen of the philosophical and/or technical problems which coaches most often raise at clinics.

Thus, *Coaching Hockey: Fundamentals, Team Play and Techniques* is a comprehensive, practical text that will assist the coach and his players from the time the first organizational meeting is called in the early fall to the end of the last game some six months later.

J. W. M.

Introduction

Amateur hockey is played under a variety of auspices and subject to many different rules and regulations. In the preparation of this text, diagrams were used which included only the essential ice markings insofar as the specific drill, play pattern or skill was concerned. A sample of this diagram, and the legend to be used in marking specific patterns, are found on p. xii.

However, at least four different sets of markings are in use today and many rinks have been designed to include two or more of these sets. The blue lines and goal lines, the corner and center-ice face-off circles are consistent from code to code. Variations do exist with respect to (a) the crease in front of each goal, (b) the restraining lines at the mid-point of the corner face-off circles and through the corner face-off spots, and (c) the center-ice line. But these minor changes affect the game to only a very small degree. The United States college hockey program operates under the N.C.A.A. rules which do *not* include any center-ice line; this allows for passing from the defensive end to the attacking blue line. This is a major change insofar as playing rules are concerned and does affect to quite a degree the use of the "fast-break" play and, as a corollary of this play, the play of the defencemen or point men when on the attack. But the absence of a center-ice line does not in any way prevent the application of the material in this text to United States college hockey coaching and playing.

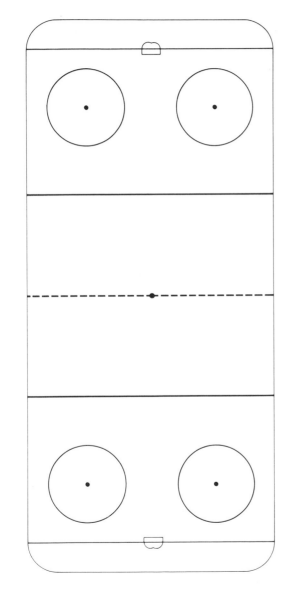

LEGEND

←—————————————	path of a skater – moving forward
←∿∿∿∿∿∿∿∿∿∿∿	path of a skater – moving backwards
←– – – – – – – –	path of a passed puck
X	player – forward or defenceman in drills – also used to identify defensive team players in pattern
D	defenceman
O	offensive player (his team has possession of the puck)
W	wing – used in play pattern
C	center – used in play pattern
①②③④⑤	used to identify player regardless of specific position because of the importance of switching in offensive and defensive hockey.
←∿∿∿————————	from forward to backward skating

COACHING HOCKEY:

Fundamentals, Team Play

and Techniques

1

Hockey Fundamentals - Checklists and Drills

INTRODUCTION

The several offensive and defensive patterns presented in Parts II and III of this manual demand a high degree of skill in skating, puckhandling, passing, shooting and checking on the part of the players. These are the five fundamental skills of hockey – prerequisites to the adoption of a successful system.

The youngest players, that is, those from eight or nine to twelve years of age, should concentrate on mastering the skills of skating, puckhandling and passing. Bantam, midget, juvenile and high school players should, as well, spend considerable time improving their abilities at shooting and checking.

Even the casual observer will note that young players commit a number of common mistakes in the performance of these fundamentals:

- they fail to turn their feet outward as they skate, thus losing power;
- they lift their heels on the recovery in skating, thus prohibiting a full-leg extension on each thrust;
- they carry their sticks too high and often swing them from side to side in "pitchfork" style;
- they fail to present a target with their stick blades when waiting for a pass;
- they concentrate too much on slap shooting despite the fact that they often have neither the strength nor the balance to execute this difficult skill correctly;

- they "slap" their passes rather than pushing them, thus reducing accuracy;
- they coast when skating corners and fail to move their centres of gravity to a location inside their feet;
- when they do get the puck, they tend to coast or glide rather than skate;
- they most often flip shoot when a good wrist shot would be preferable;
- they fail to anticipate the new location of their man when they perform a defensive check.

It has long been acknowledged that students learn best if they are presented with meaningful *cues* – simply-understood indicators on which they may focus their attention. When a player (a) has seen what should be done, (b) understands why it should be done that way, (c) is given the opportunity to practice the skill, (d) is then given direction with respect to correcting the errors committed, and, (e) in all instances, is asked to attempt a skill that is within his present capabilities, then lasting learning will result.

This first section, then, is designed to provide the coach with a list of *cues* which might be passed on to young players in the hope that they might more readily comprehend what is expected of them in the performance of the fundamental skills of hockey.

SKATING

(i) Starting - forward

(a) The heels should come together, skate blades turned outward for maximum thrust.
(b) The knees should be turned slightly outward (rather than totally forward) for maximum thrust.
(c) Both hands should be gripping the stick.
(d) The lower back should be hollow; the head should be up.
(e) The body weight should be moved forward by bending at the ankles and, to a lesser degree, at the knees.

3

(ii) The Glide – forward

(a) The drive leg should become *fully* extended while the forward leg should bend to the point that a 70-90 degree angle is formed at the knee.

(b) The head should be up, lower back hollow, trunk erect.

(c) The arms should move forward and inward slightly and backward and outward slightly.

(d) On the back swing of the arms, the elbows should come no higher than shoulder level.

(e) The skate blades should be kept parallel to the ice on the recovery.

(f) The stick blade should be kept on or near the ice; on the ice if the stick is carried in one hand, near the ice if carried in both hands.

(iii) The Stop – from forward skating

(a) The body should turn at right angles to the original direction.

(b) In turning, the head and shoulders should turn first, then the hips.

(c) The stick should be gripped in both hands.

(d) The knees should be bent so that the feet are "driven" into the ice.

(e) Body weight should be kept forward of the feet so that the greatest portion of the blades including the forward tips are driven into the ice.

(f) The back must be kept hollow, the trunk erect, the head up.

(iv) The Most Common Forward Skating Mistakes

(a) "toeing" at the start instead of turning feet outward;

(b) bending at the waist instead of at the ankles and knees;

(c) looking down at the feet;

(d) carrying the stick loosely and usually in one hand;

(e) lifting the heels upward on the recovery;

(f) swinging the arms from side to side;

(g) failing to extend the leg fully on each leg drive;

(h) toeing in to stop or sitting back on the heels when stopping.

(v) Starting – backwards

(a) The trunk must be kept erect, the head up, the lower back hollow.

(b) The knees should bend to allow the player to assume a "sit down" position.

(c) The toes should be turned inward.

(d) One hand on the stick with the grip arm straight and the blade of the stick on the ice and turned inward.

(vi) The Glide – backwards

(a) The "sitting" posture must be maintained so that the centre of gravity is behind the feet.
(b) The skate blades must remain turned inward.
(c) After each pair of thrusts, the toes of the blades should come together.
(d) The arm action should emphasize a drive backward with the elbows rising as high as shoulder-level.
(e) The head must be kept up and the back straight.

(vii) The Stop – from backward skating

(a) Two hands on the stick.
(b) The heels should come together.
(c) The knees should be turned slightly outward.
(d) The body weight should be moved forward.
(e) The trunk should be upright, the back hollow, the head up.

Note: This puts the player in the same posture as that recommended for starting forward (i).

(viii) The Most Common Backward Skating Mistakes

(a) Bending forward, looking down at the feet.
(b) Keeping two hands on the stick and pitchforking.
(c) Keeping the body weight forward instead of sitting back.
(d) "Wiggling" the ankles and feet rather than driving from the hips.
(e) Stopping with one foot rather than both feet.

(ix) Skating the Turns

(a) The stick blade should be kept on the ice and to the inside of the turn.

(b) The hips should be moved to the inside for body lean.

(c) The head and shoulders should be kept over the feet.

(d) The feet should be kept close to the ice, no heel-lifting.

(e) The inside foot should drive as the outside leg comes forward; the outside foot should drive as the inside foot is brought forward.

(x) Side-stepping

(a) The stick should be held in one hand, blade on the ice, hand close to hip.

(b) The first step should be with the leg furthest away from the desired direction.

(c) This leg should move *in front* of the other, not behind and not across.

(d) The second step should be equally short so that the original position is reassumed, then the process should be continued.

(e) Stopping should be performed on one foot, using the inside edge.

(xi) The Most Common Mistakes in Turning and Side-stepping

(a) Lifting the feet too high.
(b) Leaning the head and shoulders to the inside of a turn with the result that the feet slide away.
(c) Coasting rather than skating and skidding on the turns.
(d) Crossing the feet on side-stepping.
(e) Taking too large steps in side-stepping to the point that balance is lost.
(f) Failing to get up on the toes in side-stepping.

(xii) Turning from Forward to Backward Skating

(a) The first step should be taken with the right foot if turning to the left or the left foot if turning to the right.
(b) The step should be such that the toe of the skate blade is placed on the ice in front of the pivot foot.
(c) The foot should then be turned 180 degrees and, at the same time, the skater should stand on the toe of the pivot foot.
(d) As the player rocks down onto the full skate blade, the pivot foot is turned and executes a drive backward.
(e) In executing the turn, both hands must be on the stick and the stick should be held close to the body.
(f) As soon as the turn is completed, the stick is held out front in one hand, and the body weight is transferred backward (the backward skating position).

(xiii) Turning from Backward to Forward Skating

(a) The first step is to put both hands on the stick and hold the stick close to the body.

(b) Next, the player should lift and turn the left foot if turning to the left or the right foot if turning to the right (to the point that, for an instant, the feet are pointed in *almost* opposite directions).

(c) As the turning foot is placed on the ice, the pivot foot should turn slightly in the same direction so that it can execute a thrust in the new direction.

(d) In the execution of this skill the single most important point is to make the first step by the turning foot a very short one so that a full thrust can be exerted by the pivot foot.

(xiv) The Most Common Mistakes in Turning from Forward to Backward and Backward to Forward

(a) Forward to backward – spinning rather than stepping the turn, i.e., keeping both feet in constant contact with the ice and, through the use of upper body rotation, spinning in place, thus reducing considerably the skating speed.

(b) Backward to forward – failing to place both hands on the stick with the result that the stick ends up behind the player and out of control, and side-stepping, i.e., taking the first step with the foot furthest from the direction towards which the player wants to turn, resulting in almost complete deceleration and, oftentimes, in a fall.

Although youngsters should be encouraged to skate whenever and wherever they can, with or without sticks and protective equipment, it is clear that skating ability is often inhibited when a stick is used. It is recommended, therefore, that all skating drills be performed with sticks so that the youngsters will become thoroughly comfortable carrying this implement. It is relatively easy to develop a good arm action without a stick; it is much more difficult to achieve the same goal with one.

Skating drills should be game-like, i.e., players should be required to perform as they would in a game. Thus, a great deal of stopping and starting, changing direction and changing speed is recommended. Pucks should be included in skating drills as soon as possible since, as was indicated earlier, young players invariably slap the puck away as soon as they receive it, primarily because they have never been taught (a) to skate properly, (b) to skate with a stick, and (c) to skate carrying a puck.

PUCKHANDLING

It must be noted that young basketball players experience little difficulty in learning to dribble the ball while looking straight ahead and running. Young hockey players have not achieved nearly the same degree of competence in carrying a puck while skating with the head and eyes up. And yet this ability is as essential in hockey as dribbling is in basketball. The answer to the problem can be found only in meaningful directed practice. The following are the cues upon which the coach and his players should focus:

(i) Puckhandling – two hands on the stick

(a) The puck must be *pushed* forward and sideways, not slapped.

(b) The puck should be carried slightly back of the midpoint on the blade.

(c) The blade of the stick should be closed (that is, bent over) at the extreme points in this sideways-forward pushing of the puck.

(d) The hands should be quite close together and the pushing action should come from the wrists, not from the arms.

(e) The puck should be kept sufficiently far in front of the player that it can be seen while looking straight ahead, but not so far that it cannot be easily controlled.

(f) When skating around an opponent, the puck should be carried to the outside so that the puck-carrier's body is between the puck and the opposing player. This will require a slightly wider grip on the stick.

(ii) Puckhandling – one hand on the stick

(a) The puck should be pushed ahead with the bottom edge of the stick blade.

(b) The arm action should be a slight forward thrust by straightening the arm at the elbow.

(c) In order to keep the puck moving in a straight line, the puck should be pushed alternately with the blade pointed to the left then the right.

(d) The puck should be pushed only as far forward as will allow the player to gain instant control.

(e) As soon as the puckcarrier moves into the attacking zone or is about to be harassed by an opponent, the second hand should be placed on the stick.

(iii) The Most Common Puckhandling Mistakes

(a) Slapping the puck from side to side rather than pushing it sideways and forward.

(b) Carrying the puck at the side rather than in front of the body.

(c) Failing to close the blade over the puck when receiving a pass or pushing the puck.

(d) Using the arms rather than the wrists to propel the puck.

PASSING

Good puckhandling ability is an absolutely essential prerequisite to passing. Thus before embarking on passing drills, coaches should make certain that each player can handle a puck with a high degree of expertise. This demands that each boy have a stick that is correct for him, – right lie, right length, right weight. A lie 6 or 7 is recommended for most minor players. The length of the shaft should be such that, when the blade is on the ice, the power arm (lower hand) is straight and the fulcrum arm (upper hand) is just slightly bent. A carpenter's saw is an absolutely essential part of any coach's equipment!

Most hockey manuals devote considerable space to the many different types of passes used in hockey, but all of these are merely variations of one basic skill pattern. Perhaps too much emphasis has been placed on the development of a variety of passes and too little on those essential ingredients that are common to all passes. The following are the cues which should be transmitted to players of minor and school age:

(i) Delivering the Pass

(a) The puck should be cradled on the blade slightly to the rear of center of the blade.

(b) The whole blade should be in contact with the ice – not just the heel or toe.

(c) The blade should be closed over the puck to increase control.

(d) Delivery should begin well behind the passer so that full acceleration is achieved by the time the stick blade reaches the point that it is at right angles to the desired direction of the pass.

(e) The puck should be released (pushed) at a point where the blade is at right angles to the desired direction.

(f) The passer should then follow-through low and with a closed blade in the case of regular passes, slightly higher and with an open blade in the case of raised or flip passes.

(g) The weight should be transferred from the rear to the forward foot as the puck is moved forward.

(h) The passer's eyes should be fixed on the target presented by his teammate's stick blade.

(ii) Receiving the Pass

(a) The potential receiver should present a target with his stick blade – a target that is at right angles to the direction of the pass.
(b) As the puck approaches the target, the receiver should move his blade towards the puck to receive it and then "give" with the pass as he closes his blade to assure retention and control.

(iii) Leading the Receiver

(a) The passer must anticipate the receiver's position and pass to that spot.
(b) Because of the tendency to look down at the puck when receiving, which makes the receiver vulnerable for a check, it is important that the passer *not* lead his teammate into this kind of trouble.
(c) Passes that fall short of the mark can be retrieved on the skate blades and kicked forward to the stick.
(d) Passes that hit the boards will rebound at an angle equal and opposite to that of the approach; their direction should therefore be anticipated.

(iv) Major Passing Mistakes

(a) Failing to push the pass; slapping the puck instead.
(b) Failing to lead the receiver.
(c) Looking down at the puck rather than up and at the target.
(d) Leading the receiver into a check.
(e) Passing too softly.
(f) Starting passes in front of rather than beside and behind the body.

SHOOTING

(v) Major Receiving Mistakes

(a) Failing to set up a target with the stick blade.
(b) Failing to hold the target at right angles to the direction of the pass.
(c) Failing to cushion the pass reception, thus allowing the puck to carom off the blade.
(d) Failing to practice receiving passes on the backhand as well as the forehand.

The "bread and butter" skill of hockey is shooting–and scoring, and, as such, one cannot minimize the importance of this fundamental skill. It is sad to note, however, that the large majority of young players consume most of their shooting practice time on slap shots without ever achieving either accuracy or quickness of delivery. There are many different shooting deliveries: the wrist shot, the short slap or snap shot, the flip shot, the slap shot, the deflection. Each has its place in hockey but coaches should attempt to get their players to concentrate more on accuracy and quickness of delivery and less on "booming" shots off the boards, screen or protective glass! Backhand shooting has become an almost forgotten art although a few star players are beginning to ressurect these shots as important parts of their skill repertoires. With minor and school players, shooting techniques can be divided into two main categories: forehand and backhand wrist shots, and snap and short slap shots. The following are the essential ingredients of each:

(i) Forehand and Backhand Wrist Shots

(a) The puck must be brought back to the side and behind the shooter as the first part of the delivery; wrist shots should *not* begin in front of the shooter.

(b) The player's eyes should be on the goal, not on the puck.

(c) The puck should be brought forward vigorously with the blade closed over the puck and held firmly on the ice surface.

(d) The release should be made at a point when the stick blade is at right angles to the desired direction of the shot.

(e) The follow-through should, in the case of wrist shots, be low with the blade turning over the puck, and, in the case of flip shots, high, with the blade turning under the puck.

(f) The body weight should be transferred from the rear to the forward foot in the process of delivering the puck.

20

(ii) The Snap or Short Slap Shot

(a) The puck should be set to the forehand side and slightly in front of the shooter.

(b) The upper body should be turned sideways with the weight evenly distributed on both feet.

(c) The wrists should be "cocked" and the stick blade brought back to the point that the tip of the blade is not higher than knee level.

(d) On the back swing, the blade should be closed.

(e) On the down swing, the blade should hit the ice immediately behind the puck so that the upper portion of the blade is actually hitting down on the puck.

(f) The follow-through should be short and violent as the wrists uncock.

(g) In the process of shooting, the player should keep his eyes focused on the goal.

Note: In executing the full slap shot, the only two differences are:
- the eyes are focused on the puck throughout the delivery, and
- the follow-through is long and low with the blade turned over the puck as in the wrist shot.

(iii) The Most Common Shooting Mistakes

(a) Looking down at the puck rather than up and at the goal.
(b) Relying too much on the more "dramatic" slap shot.
(c) Starting wrist shots from in front of the body, thus invariably shooting the puck too far to the left or right.
(d) Stickhandling the puck rather than shooting as soon as it is received.
(e) Shooting off the rear foot, resulting in shots that are too high.
(f) Failing to follow the shot in towards the goal for rebounds.
(g) Shooting at the goaltender.
(h) Shooting too high (most goals are scored within six inches of the ice surface).

Because considerable emphasis has been placed on (a) looking at the goal not the puck, and (b) uncocking the wrists in shooting, it follows that two essential prerequisites to good shooting are: (a) a high degree of ability at puckhandling, and (b) strong wrists, hands and fingers. The coach is urged to devote considerable time to puckhandling practice and to hand strength exercises (cf. Part VI – Conditioning).

CHECKING

The skill of checking, that is, the technique of moving the man away from the puck and, occasionally, the puck away from the man, is perhaps the most difficult one to teach since it cannot be broken down into smaller, more easily digestible parts. Once the player is given the concept and shown the technique, only directed practice at full speed and under competitive conditions will produce the desired results.

Slow motion checking drills are *not* recommended because they can result in injury to one or the other combatant. Every precaution must be exercised by the coach with respect to keeping sticks low and blades on or near the ice. Far too many checks involve cross-checking, high sticking, spearing – all serious game infractions as well as potentially dangerous procedures. The severity of a check is not nearly as important as its effectiveness in "tying-up" the puckcarrier.

(i) The Most Important Cues

(a) Always keep two hands on the stick in the process of checking.

(b) The final few steps before applying the check should be controlled ones in the event that a change of direction is required.

(c) The point of aim should be the puckcarrier's chest.

(d) The boards and goal should be used to advantage as factors which reduce the number of direction options open to the puckcarrier.

(e) In making contact, pressure should be applied in such a way that the puckcarrier's arms and stick are "pinned" against the boards.

(f) The follow-up to the initial check should be such that the puckcarrier's feet are immobilized to prevent him from kicking the puck to a teammate.

(g) The position assumed by the checker should be such that he can easily roll away from his check and pick up the puck.

(h) It is considerably easier to move the puckcarrier in the same direction as he was going when the check was applied than in the opposite direction; in other words, the checker should use the puckcarrier's momentum to advantage.

(i) Regardless of the success of the check, the checker should maintain contact as long as is legally possible to prevent the puckcarrier from returning to the play.

(j) In the case of stick-checking (poke-checking, sweep-checking, etc.), the key is to get as close to the puckcarrier as possible so that the initial stick-check can, if necessary, be followed up with a body check.

(k) Body checking at the points should *always* take the form of a jamming type of check; hip checks are *always* inappropriate and dangerous procedures at the points.

(l) In applying checks on 1 on 1 and 2 on 2 situations, defencemen should take advantage of the defensive blue line in that a well applied check can force an off-side.

(m) Because players do often look down in the process of receiving a pass or shooting, solid checks can effectively be applied at this point.

(n) Stick-checks should *never* be used on players who are in the process of passing, receiving a pass, or shooting; body checks should always be used in these situations.

(ii) The Most Common Mistakes in Checking

(a) "Running" at a check, i.e., skating too fast and out of control.

(b) Lunging at a check, i.e., throwing the body forward and off-balance.

(c) Reaching for a check, i.e., attempting to check the opponent with the stick by reaching forward instead of skating close enough to follow-up with a proper body check.

(d) Concentrating too much on the puck and not sufficiently on the man.

(e) Checking the opponent from the rear, thus allowing him to elude the check.

(f) Hip-checking instead of shoulder-checking.

(g) Failing to maintain contact with a check long enough.

(h) Failing to maintain body or stick contact with a check in front of the goal.

The five fundamentals of hockey – skating, puck-handling, passing, shooting and checking – can be mastered with time, practice and patience. But it is important for the coach to be able to say to one of his charges, "This is not working well for you because . . .", and then, "Here is what you should concentrate on doing in the future . . .". The 103 cues presented in this section should assist the coach in this process. A word of caution is essential here. It would be sheer folly to have the player concentrate on too many cues at any one time. Coaches are advised to watch the player perform, isolate the key error or errors, identify these for the player, suggest ways of eliminating them, and then direct him in his correct practice of the technique. But this can occur only if the coach is aware of the many cues that might be suggested.

HOCKEY DRILLS

Twenty-four drills designed to improve skill ability at skating, puckhandling, passing, shooting and checking, are included for possible use by coaches. It must be stressed that these represent only a small cross-section of the many drills available to coaches who agree that *all* drills should really be excerpts from the game itself. In point of fact, each of the situations and patterns included in Parts II and III of this manual can and should be used as drills. However, many coaches may find it necessary to "zero-in" on one specific fundamental, and these rather simple mass activity drills have been designed to do just that.

In the Appendix, a sample drill sheet of each type is provided for reproduction so that coaches might add their own drills, in the hope that this book may thus become more personal, and therefore more useful.

In a number of the drills illustrated, use has been made of plastic pylons which are available from some sporting goods and all safety supply stores. These are most useful in that they can be used to divide the ice into sections, and provide targets for passing and shooting, thus assisting the coach in setting up challenges insofar as the development of basic puckhandling ability is concerned.

In a few instances use has been made of extra goals in the neutral zone. It is felt that far too little time is spent on the development of goaltending skills; thus, any move which will increase the amount of goaler participation and practice time surely is worthwhile. If the neutral zone is *not* being used to advantage then it seems logical to provide extra shooting-goaling practice stations in that location.

Finally, all passing drills emphasize carrying the puck out and in the alleys, the basic technique upon which all offensive hockey is based. In no instance should a drill contradict the basic principles which the coach is attempting to promote.

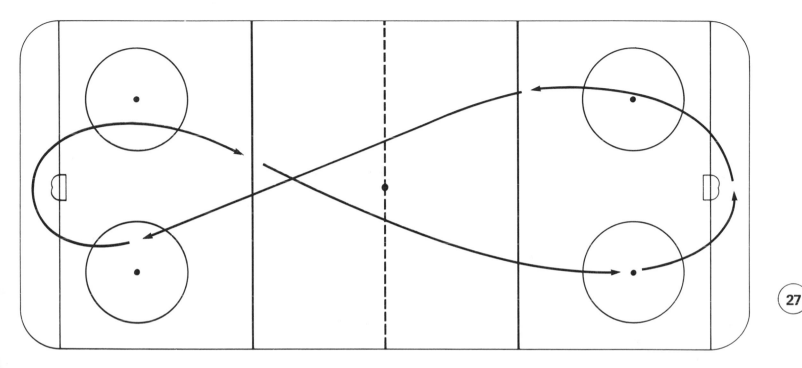

1. Figure 8 – skating (and puckhandling)

- with or without pucks
- forwards and backwards
- combining warm-up exercises with skating.

27

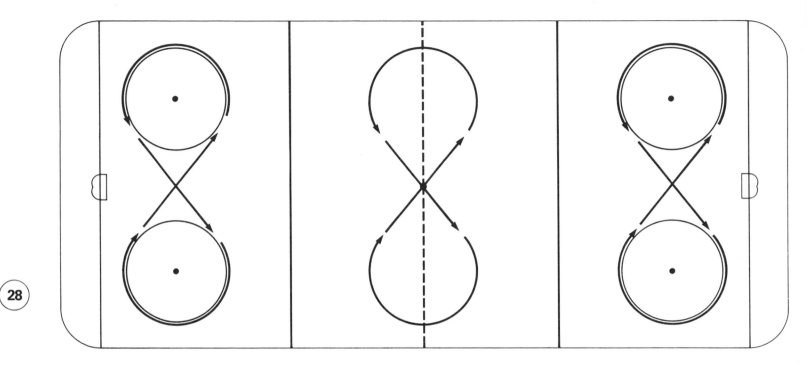

2. Small Figure 8 – skating the turns

–   with or without pucks.

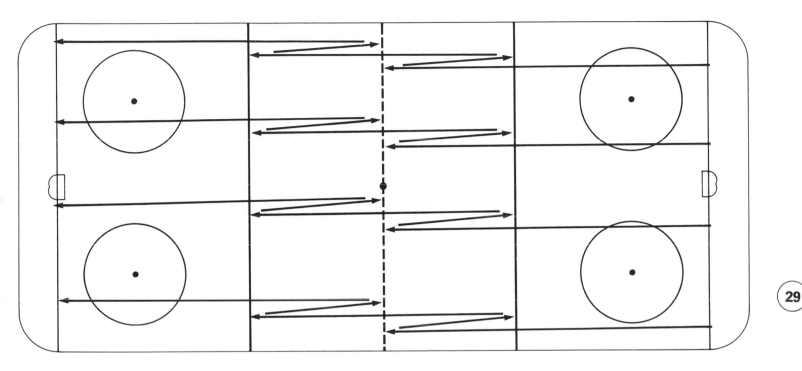

3. Lightning Drill – endurance

- skating forward or combining forward and backward skating (especially good at the end of a practice).

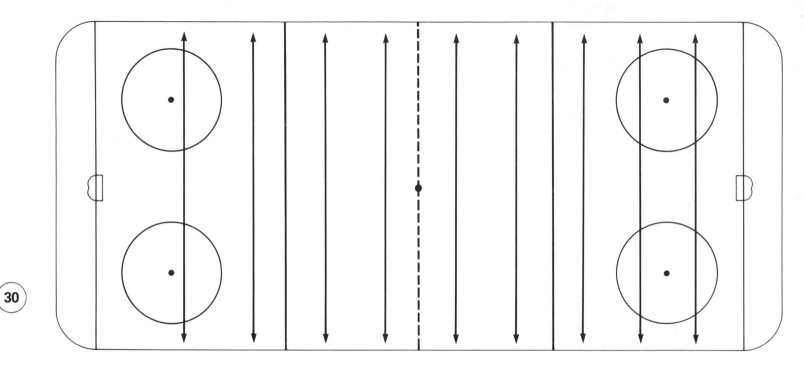

4. Across and back – speed and stopping

- alone or in pairs
- forward or backward
- pushing or pulling partner.

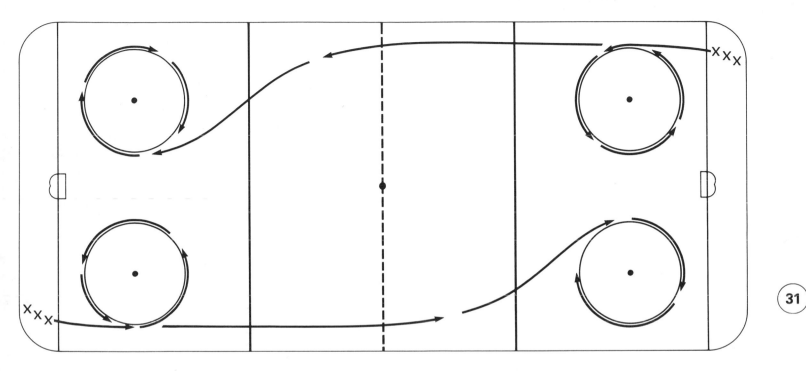

5. Skating and Puckhandling

- on circles
- through neutral zone
- break-in.

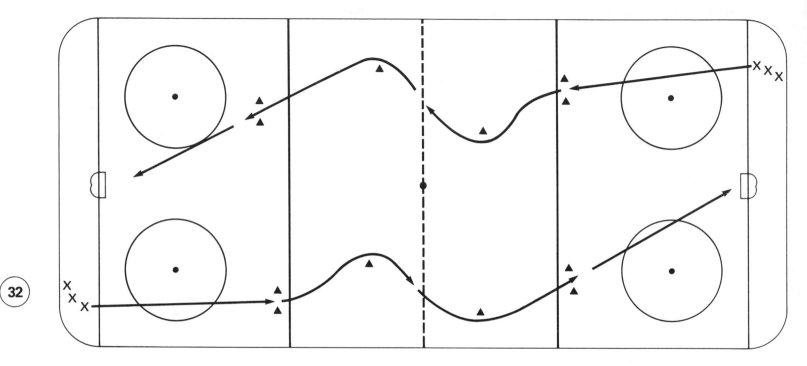

6. Skating and Puckhandling Using Pylons

32

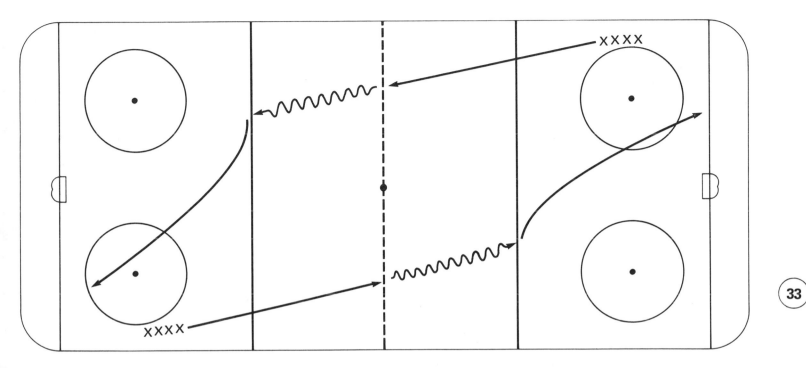

7. Forward and Backward Cutting Drill

- forward to red line
- backwards to blue line
- cut and forward to corner.

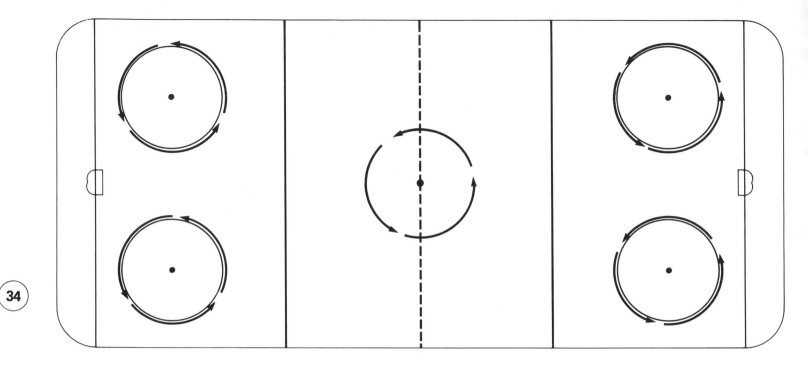

34

8. Skating the Circles

- in both directions with or without pucks.

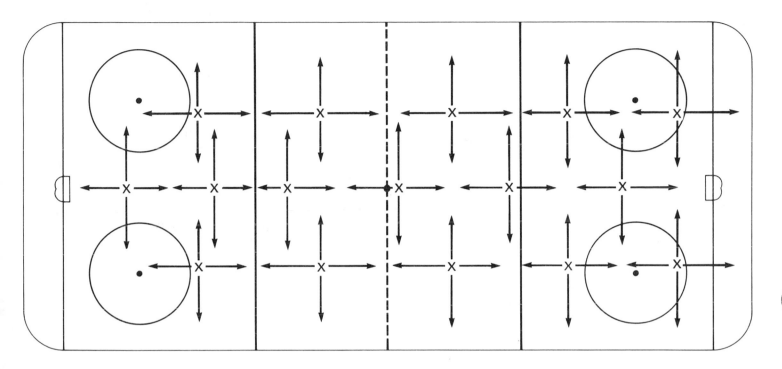

9. Skating Agility Drill

- forward
- backward
- side-step, left and right.

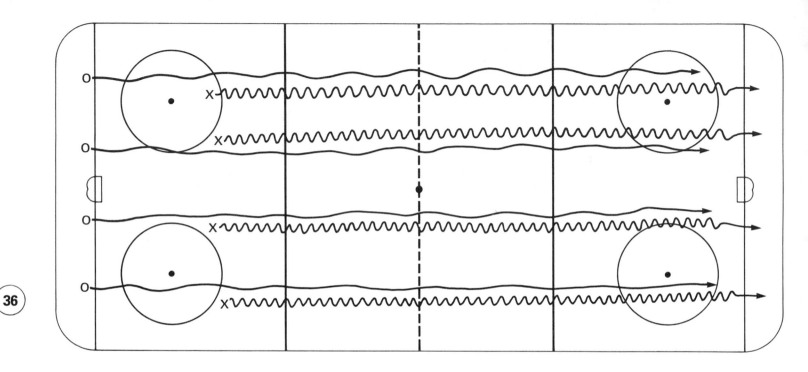

36

10. One Against One

0 – skating forward
X – skating backwards
– with or without pucks.

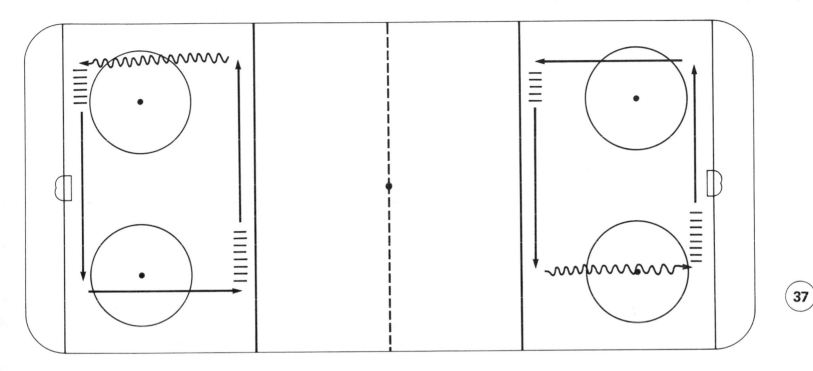

11. Skating the Square

- forward to side-step to forward to backward to
  side-step to forward.

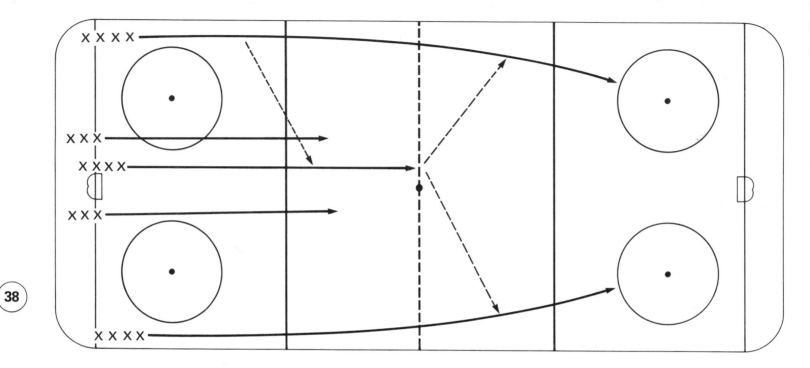

12. Five vs. None Skating – puckhandling and passing drill

- add 1 defender, then 2, then 3, etc., as ability
  improves.

38

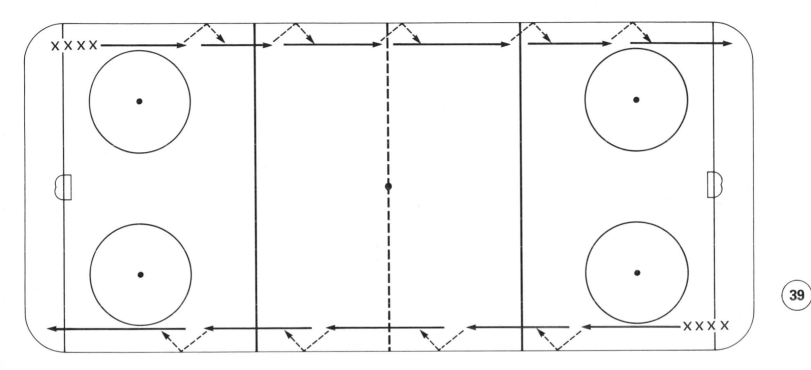

13. Skating and Puckhandling Drill

- players skate down the ice passing the puck
  against the boards and retrieving these passes on
  their sticks and skates.

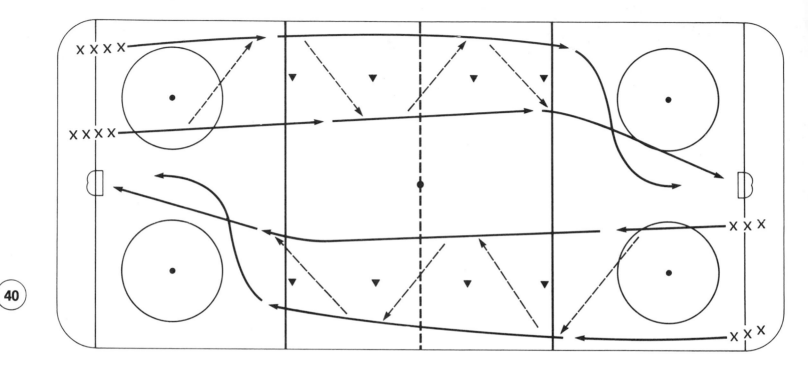

14. Skating – puckhandling and passing and shooting

- in pairs, passing the puck between pylons and breaking for the goal.

40

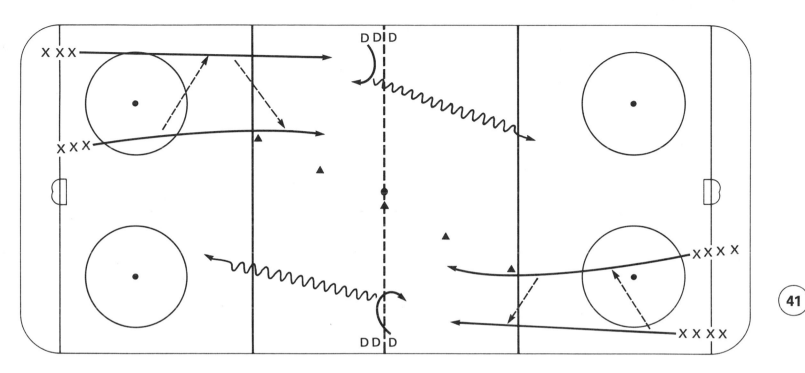

15. Two on One

- passing, checking, shooting
- ice divided into sections by diagonal pylons.

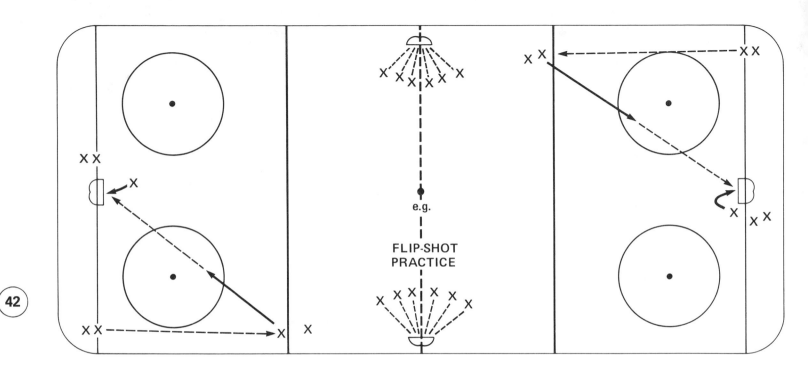

**FLIP-SHOT
PRACTICE**

16. Passing – Shooting – Deflecting

- note: additional drills can be conducted in
  neutral zone at the same time.

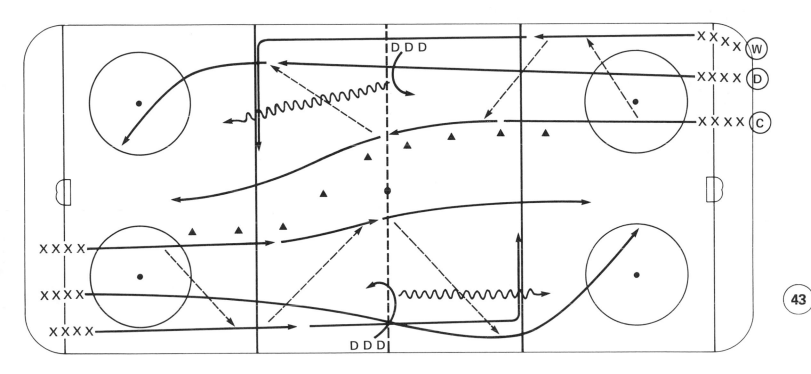

17. Two on One with delayed defenceman

- wing-up the alley and cut
- center-up the inside alley
- defenceman-delay and break in offensive alley.

43

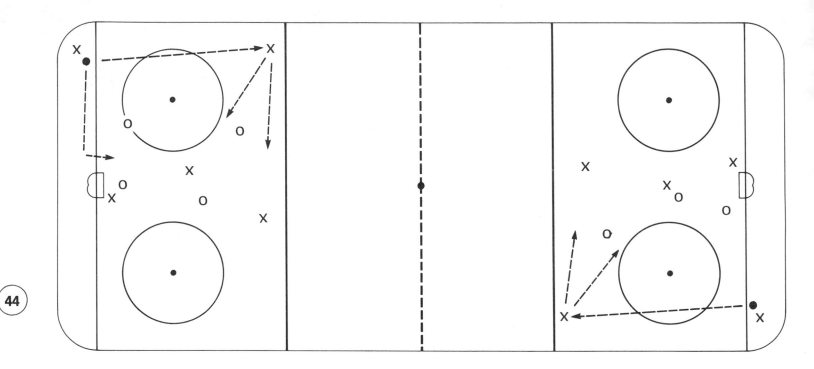

18. Power Play Drill

- passing, shooting, checking
- 5 against 2, 3, 4.

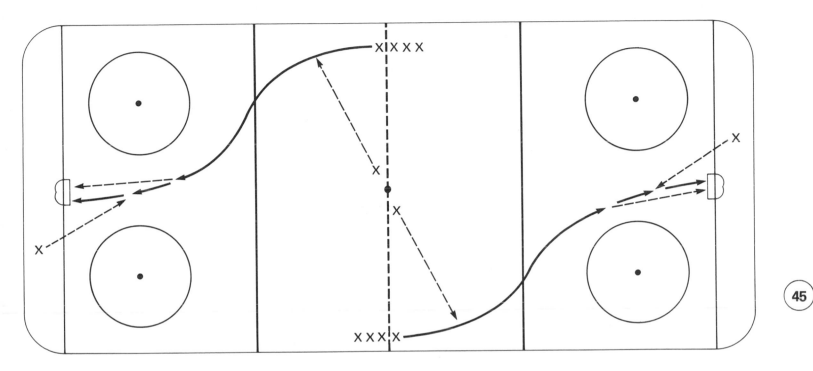

19. Rebounding Drill

- as shot is made, a second puck is passed out
  from behind the goal.

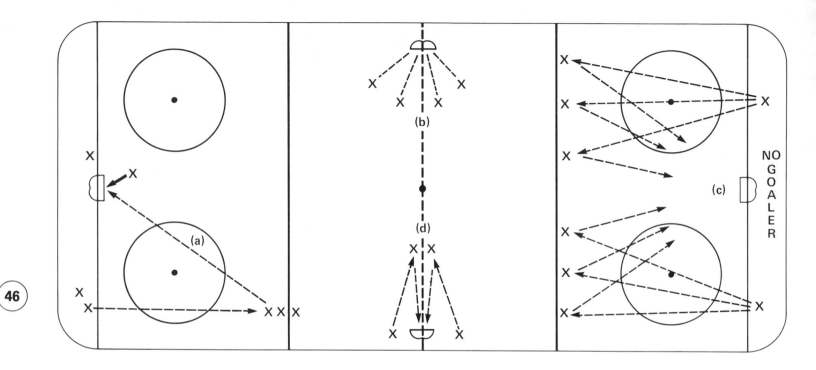

20. Multi-Station Shooting Drill

(a) – point and deflections
(b) – flip shots
(c) – slap shots
(d) – wrist shots from slot.

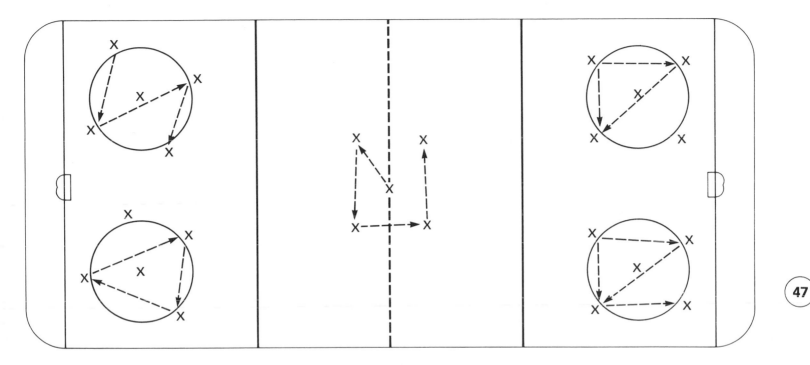

21. Passing – Reacting Drill

- one player in the center of each circle.
- teammates pass the puck back and forth; he tries to intercept.
- difficulty is increased by having passers skate around the circle while passing.

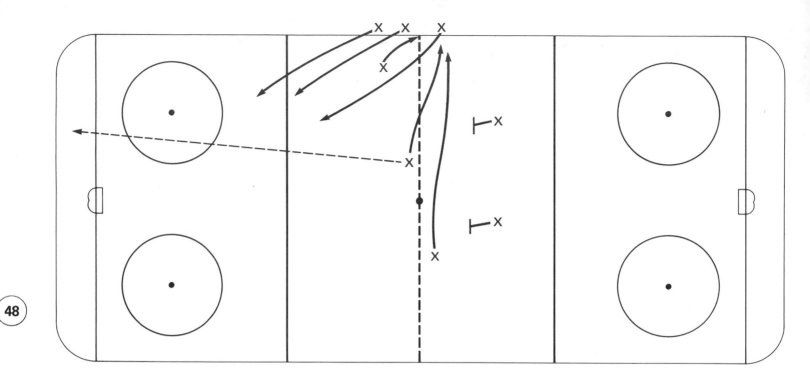

22. Changing-on-the-Fly Drill

- team X tries to get puck across red line, shoot it into attacking zone and change the forward line on the move.

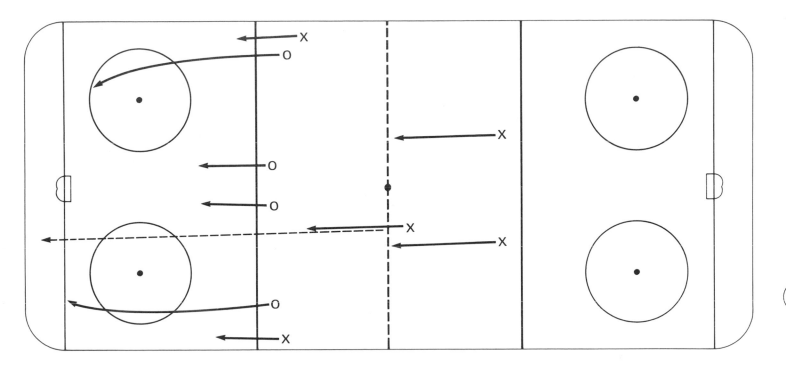

23. Forechecking Drill – Four against Five

- puck is shot into the defensive zone from center ice.

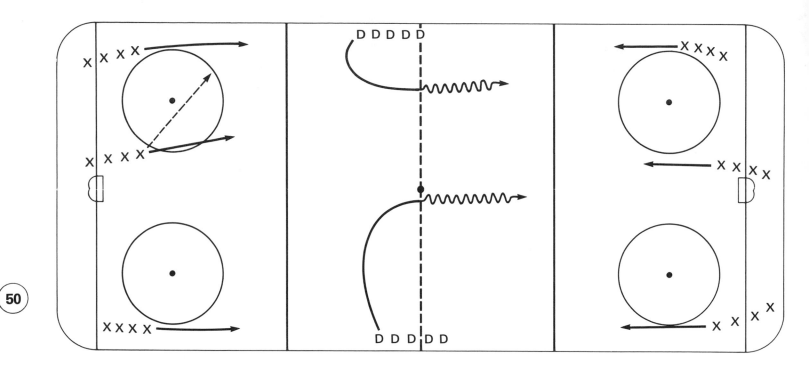

24. Three on Two Passing and Checking Drill –
working from both ends

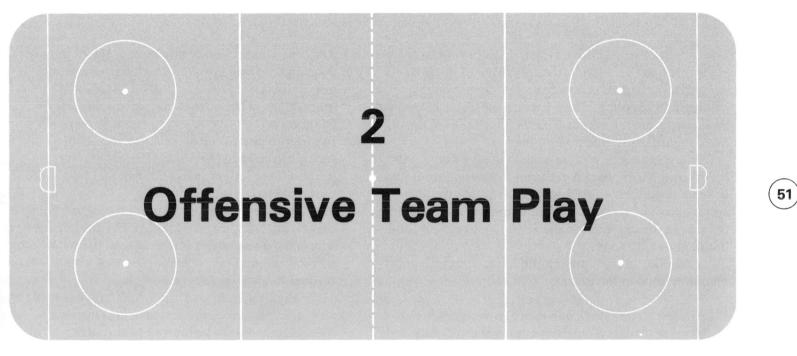

2
Offensive Team Play

INTRODUCTION

The object of an offensive system in hockey is to score goals through the organized application of the fundamental individual skills of skating, puckhandling, passing and shooting. Thus, pattern offensive play must begin the moment a team secures possession of the puck regardless of position on the ice.

Since possession can be achieved anywhere on the ice – through forechecking, through pass interceptions or from scrambles – it follows that a sound offensive system must be so devised that it applies anywhere on the ice: in the defensive zone, in the neutral zone, and in the attacking zone.

A number of preliminary and basic principles must be understood at the outset:

(a) Since a passed puck can move more quickly than a skating player, offensive personnel must constantly attempt to "head man" the puck, that is, to pass it up-ice to breaking players.

(b) In order to elude defensive checks it is essential to "load" a zone, that is, to force the opposition to attempt to check two players with one, or three with two, or four with three. By so doing, one offensive player should always be free to receive a pass.

(c) The best areas to use coming out of the defensive zone and moving into the attacking zone are the alleys – the areas bounded by the boards and the inner edges of the corner face-off circles (cf. Diagram A).

(d) In order to guarantee (as much as is possible) success in passing the puck, short passes are preferable to longer ones and diagonal passes are preferred to lateral ones.

(e) The safest and most logical place to begin offensive plays from one's own zone is from behind the net where the puckcarrier is free to scan the whole ice surface and make intelligent judgments with respect to initial passes or moves.

(f) Since the best location from which to score is the area defined as the slot (the area measuring approximately ten feet wide and twenty-five feet deep in front of the opposition's goal), the offensive patterns must be so devised that they open this area by attracting defencemen away from the slot (cf. Diagram B).

(g) Most successful shots on goal are directed from the offensive points (cf. Diagram C).

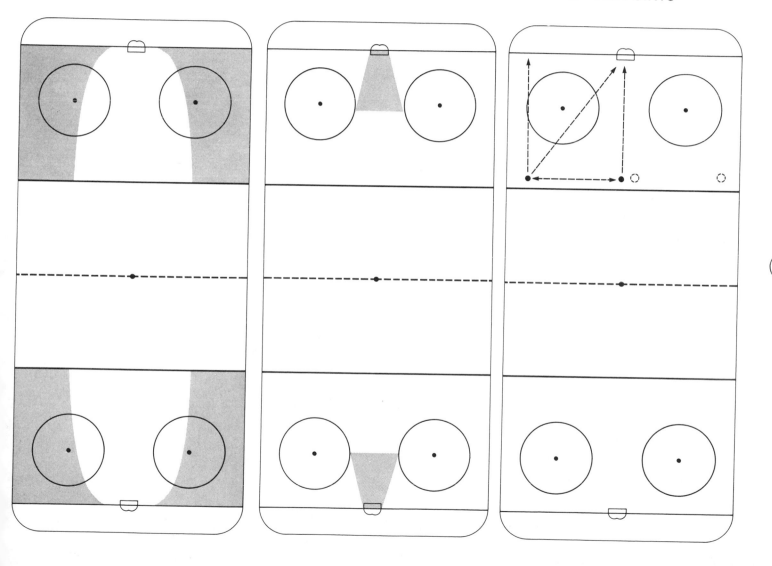

A. "ALLEYS"

B. "SLOT"

C. "THE POINTS"

53

OFFENSIVE PATTERNS — COMING OUT OF THE DEFENSIVE ZONE

The following patterns may be employed to move the puck out of the defensive zone. Note: All patterns can work to the left or to the right.

1. Defenceman has possession behind goal.
   Wings have both come back to deep positions.
   Center takes up position in slot.
   Defenceman passes to wing who starts out up-ice.
   Wing passes to center who has wheeled.
   Pattern continues as a 3-2 rush.

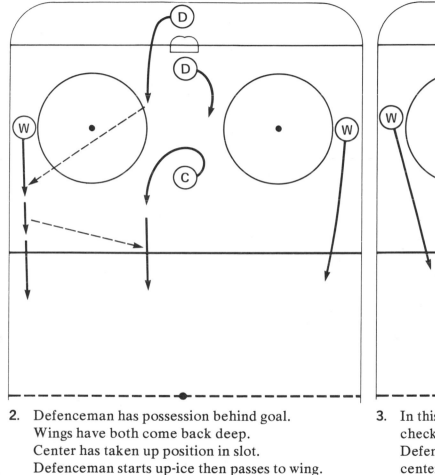
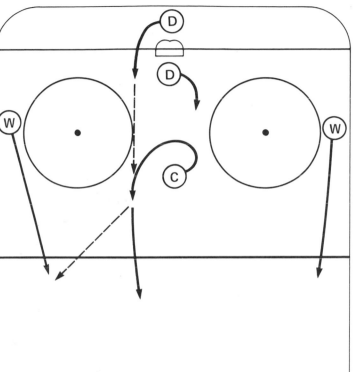

2. Defenceman has possession behind goal.
Wings have both come back deep.
Center has taken up position in slot.
Defenceman starts up-ice then passes to wing.
Wing passes to center who has wheeled.
Pattern continues as a 3-2 rush.

3. In this situation, starting the same as the above, the
checkers have covered the wings.
Defenceman passes the puck up to the wheeling
center.
Center then passes to wing who has escaped his
check.
Pattern continues as a 3-2 rush.

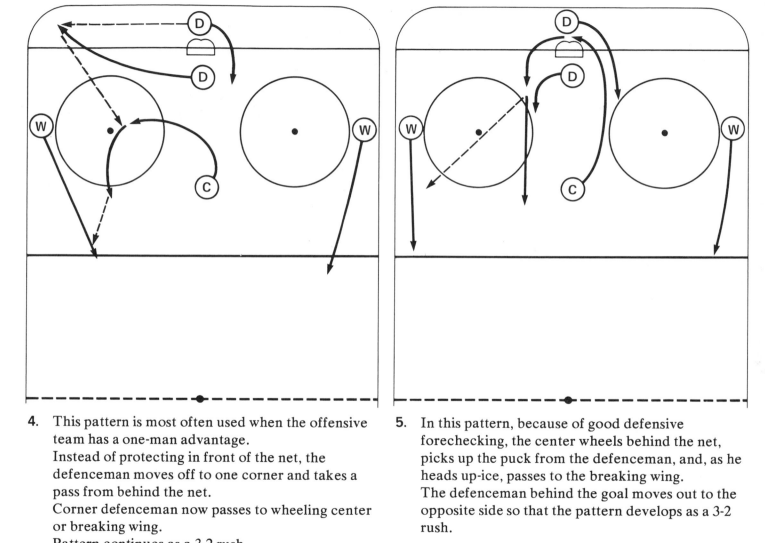

4. This pattern is most often used when the offensive team has a one-man advantage.

    Instead of protecting in front of the net, the defenceman moves off to one corner and takes a pass from behind the net.

    Corner defenceman now passes to wheeling center or breaking wing.

    Pattern continues as a 3-2 rush.

5. In this pattern, because of good defensive forechecking, the center wheels behind the net, picks up the puck from the defenceman, and, as he heads up-ice, passes to the breaking wing.

    The defenceman behind the goal moves out to the opposite side so that the pattern develops as a 3-2 rush.

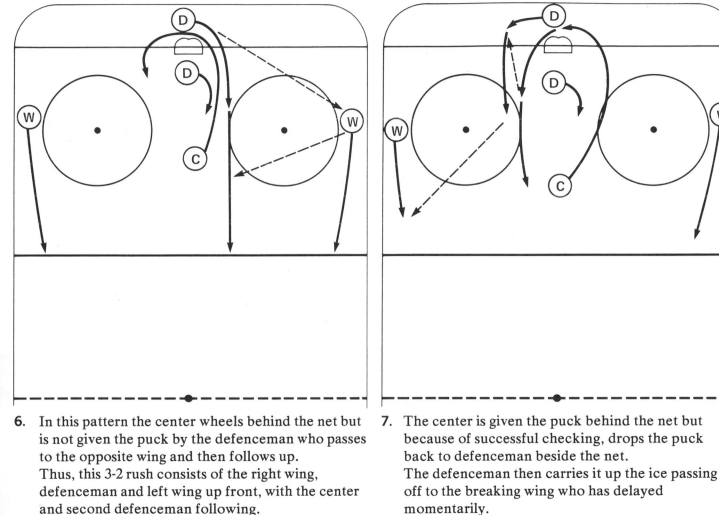

6. In this pattern the center wheels behind the net but is not given the puck by the defenceman who passes to the opposite wing and then follows up.

Thus, this 3-2 rush consists of the right wing, defenceman and left wing up front, with the center and second defenceman following.

7. The center is given the puck behind the net but because of successful checking, drops the puck back to defenceman beside the net.

The defenceman then carries it up the ice passing off to the breaking wing who has delayed momentarily.

The center takes over as one of the two trailing players on this 3-2 rush.

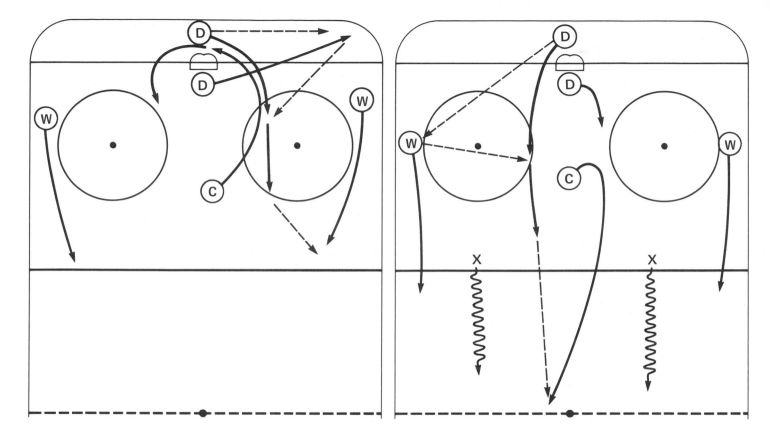

8. In this pattern the center who wheels behind the goal is *not* given the puck because of forechecking. As the center pulls up in front of the net, the other defenceman moves off to the corner to take the pass.

Here is created a give-and-go situation in that one defenceman passes to the second who gives it back to the first.

9. Occasionally, that is, when a defensive team tends to concentrate more on backchecking than on forechecking, the defenceman or center can skate up-ice with the puck and pass to a breaking player between and beyond the opposing defenceman.

This diagram illustrates the pattern in which a defenceman passes to a breaking center.

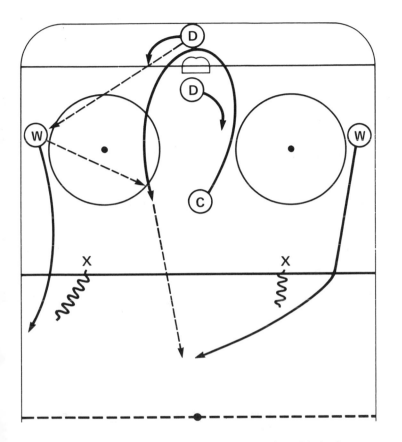

10. This diagram illustrates the pattern in which the center passes to a breaking wing.

Basic Patterns – The Neutral Zone

Once an offensive team has succeeded in working the puck out of its defensive zone, the secret of good pattern hockey is to move the puck into the center alley of the neutral zone

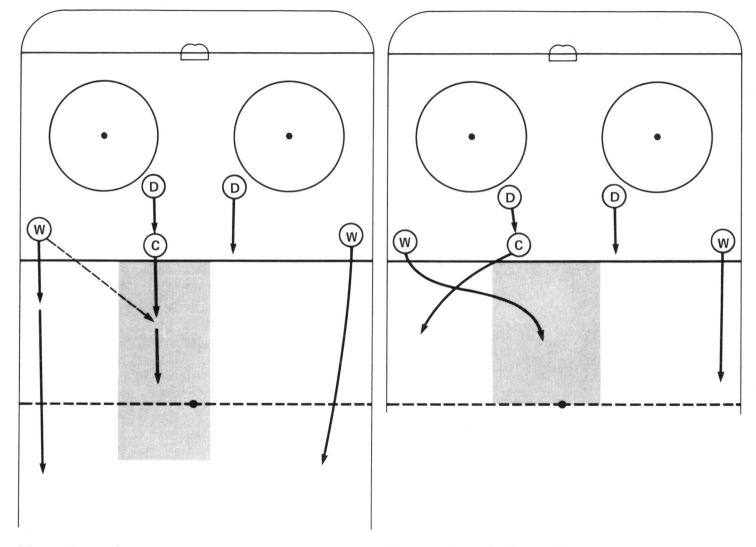

60

11. . . . by passing

12. . . . or by switching positions.

OFFENSIVE PLAY IN THE DEFENSIVE ZONE:

GOALERS

Gain control of the puck shot into your end zone and set it up for your teammate behind your goal and about one foot from the end boards.

When a teammate has possession of the puck behind your goal, take up a position on the post nearest the location of the puck in the event that a miscue is committed.

Always be prepared to receive a back pass from a defenceman or center in the event that fore-checkers inhibit their movement up the ice.

Try to assist your teammates by providing verbal directions or assistance in the process of setting up an offensive pattern.

DEFENCEMEN

Don't "run" for the back of the goal unless it is necessary; if you can secure the puck and immediately begin an offensive pattern, then do so.

When you do have possession of the puck behind your own net, take up a position slightly off-center so that your goaler can establish himself on one or the other of the goal posts.

Keep moving the puck so that you will not force the play to be stopped for a delaying face-off.

Make your passes crisp; speed is of the essence in getting out of your own end.

Remember that the "give and go" play is the most successful one in hockey today; every time you deliver a pass, move up the ice as a possible target for a return pass.

Follow the play out of your own end and do not remain further behind the puck than half a zone.

WINGS

As soon as a teammate gains possession of the puck, move deep into your own end – certainly as deep as the face-off circle hash-mark, and occasionally as deep as the goal line.

Always face the net; never allow yourself to end up facing the sideboards.

Give a target with your stick and allow your stick to move forward to meet the pass.

Once you start your move out of your own end, skate as fast as you possibly can.

CENTERS

Keep moving in the slot; don't stand still waiting for the play to develop.

If two or more opposing players are forechecking, be ready to wheel around the net.

If a defence player slides off to a corner, move towards the goal before wheeling in order to cover the front of the net in the event of a miscue.

If a wing or defenceman moves into the center alley, be ready either to drop back as a defenceman or to swing to the open wing.

The process of moving the puck out of the defensive zone is a reasonably simple one *if* players understand that the *puck* must do the moving rather than the player.

As soon as the puckcarrier has established himself in the center lane of the neutral zone, it then becomes important to put into action the second phase of the offensive system – the phase that hopefully will lead directly or indirectly to a goal. The following patterns are suggested. Note: In all illustrations, patterns have been developed to the right side; they should be practised to the left as well.

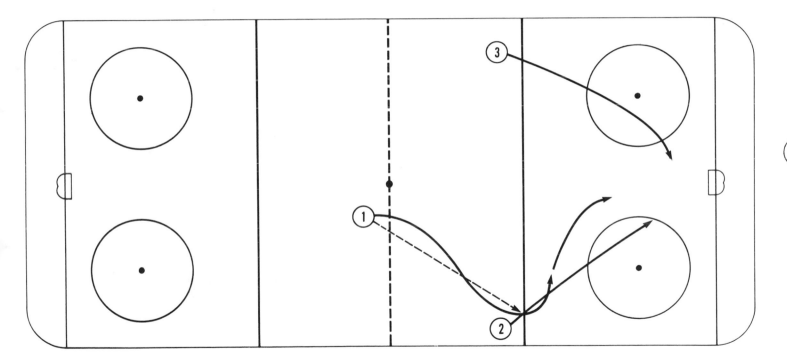

63

13. ① passes to ② breaking in at the blue line.
    ② heads directly for the slot.
    ③ heads for the left post to deflect or rebound.
    ① proceeds to the slot for rebounds after trailing ② .

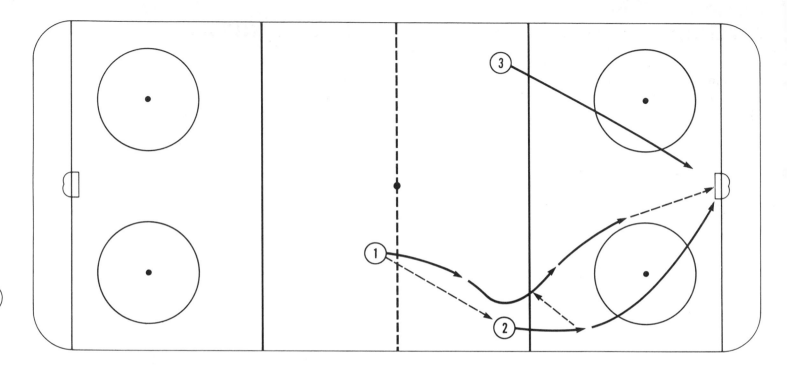

14. ① passes to ② breaking in at the blue line and trails.
② drop passes to ① inside the blue line and heads for the post.
③ breaks in for the left post.
① cuts into the slot for the shot.
② and ③ are in position to deflect or rebound.

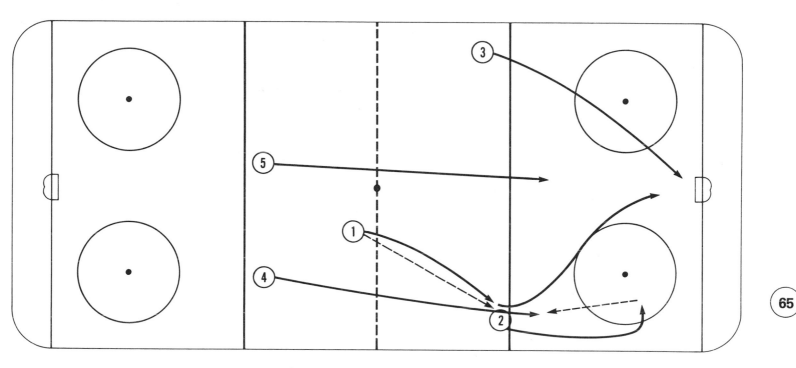

15. ① passes to ② breaking in at the blue line and trails.
② skates in as far as the hash mark on the face-off
circle.
① breaks for the slot.
③ breaks in for the left post.
④ follows up to point position for pass back from ② .
⑤ takes up position at left point.

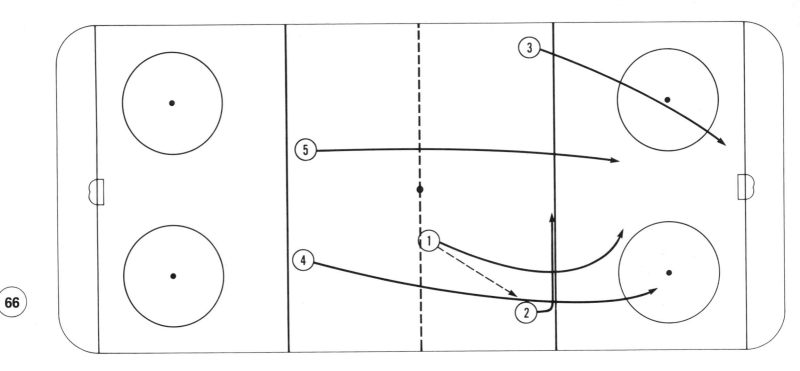

16. ② fails to receive pass so straddles offensive blue line.
④ immediately follows up in right alley.
① passes to ④ behind screen established by ②.
③ breaks for the left post.

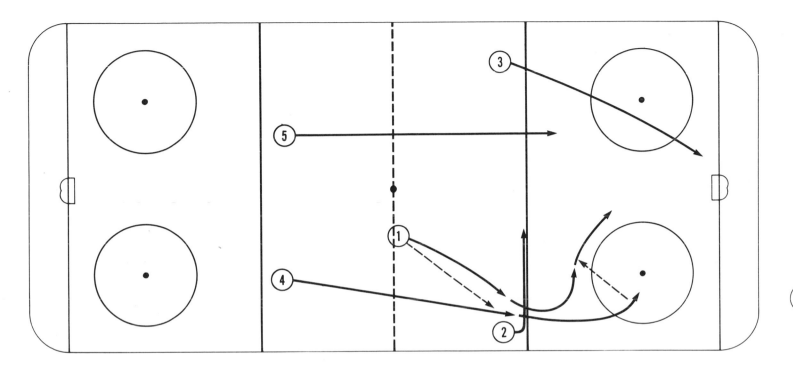

17. This pattern is a variation of No. 16 in that ④ skates to center of face-off circle, passes back to ① who cuts for the slot and the shot.

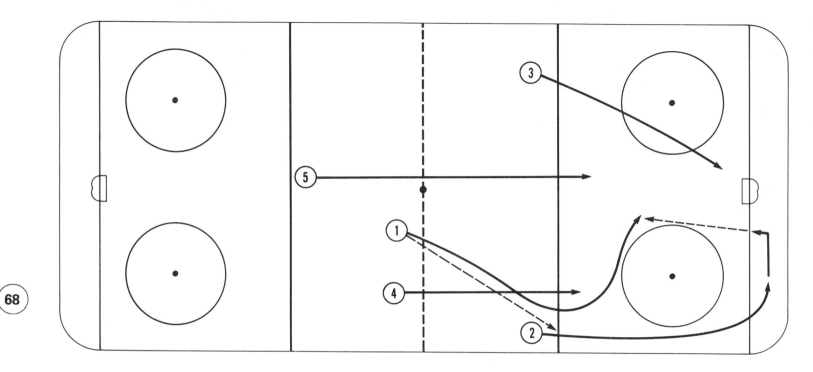

18. ① passes to ② at the offensive blue line.
② fails to drop pass or pass back to point so continues around corner to side of goal.
② passes out to ① who has trailed and moves into slot.

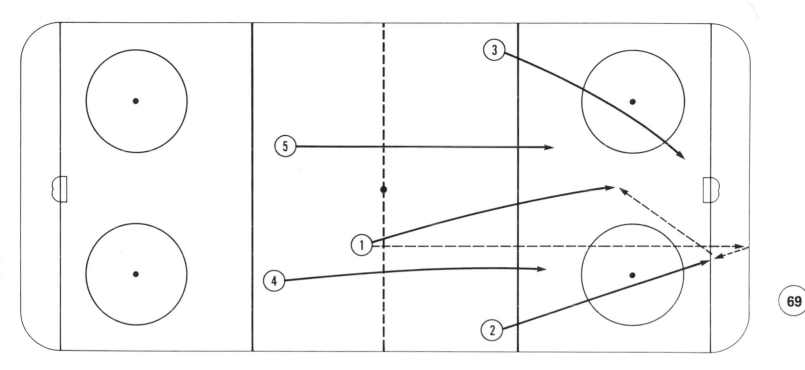

19. ① is unable to make pass to ② or ③ so fires the puck
into offensive zone about 10 to 15 feet off the net.
② races in to pick up carom from end boards.
③ takes up left post position.
④ and ⑤ move up to point positions.
① follows in to slot for pass out from ② .

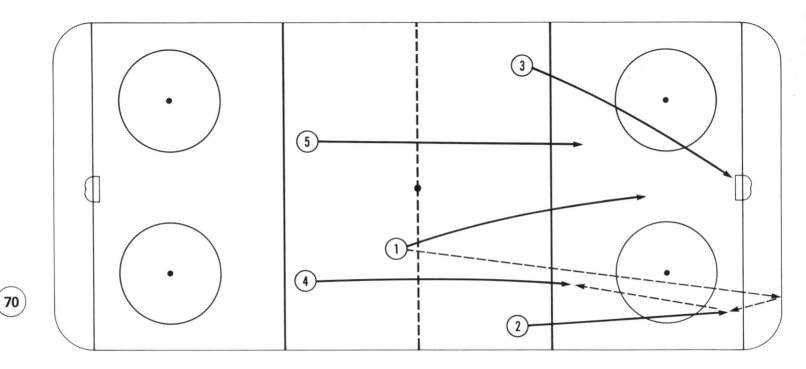

20. ① fails to pass to ② or ③ at offensive blue line and cannot shoot puck straight to end boards. He shoots slightly at an angle to the outside.

② races in to pick up carom near side boards and passes back to ④ who has moved into right point position.

④ moves towards net for shot or exercises other point options:
- pass to opposite point
- shot off goal for deflection
- pass back to corner
- pass into the slot.

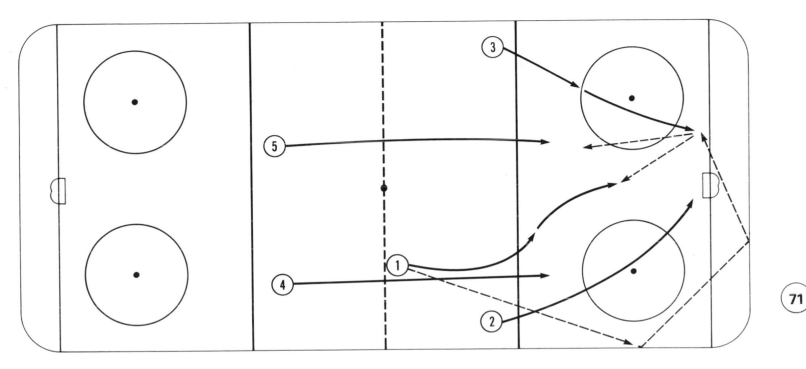

21. Again ① fails to complete breaking pass to ② or ③ and
cannot (because of checkers) shoot just off the goal.
He shoots puck towards near corner so that it
caroms around behind net where it is picked up by ③
who then feeds it to ① , who has moved into slot, or
back to ⑤ at the left point.

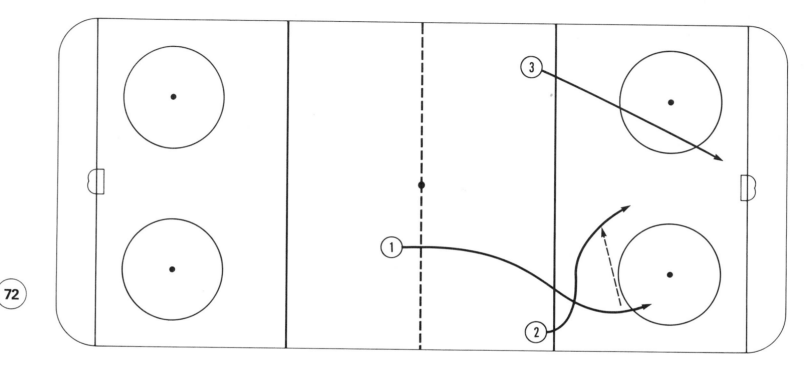

22. The puckcarrier finds himself slightly ahead of his wings and thus unable to complete a pass diagonally forward. He crosses blue line, fades for the side alley, and passes to his wing who has delayed and moved towards the slot. This is a simple switch between ① and ② .

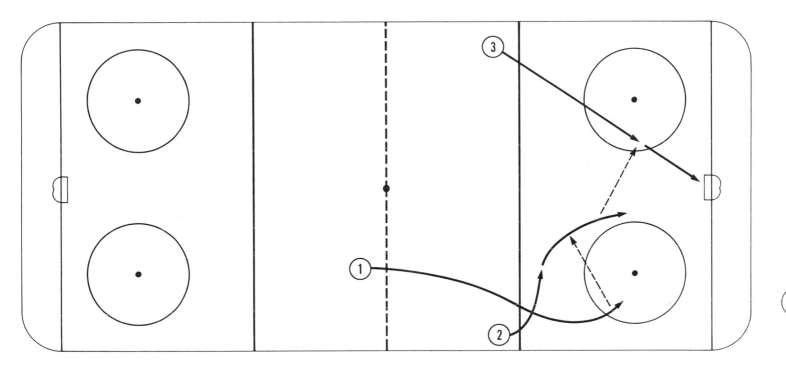

23. This is an extension of No. 22 in that, after receiving the puck near the blue line, ② passes it over to ③ who moves in for the shot; ② follows up for the rebound.

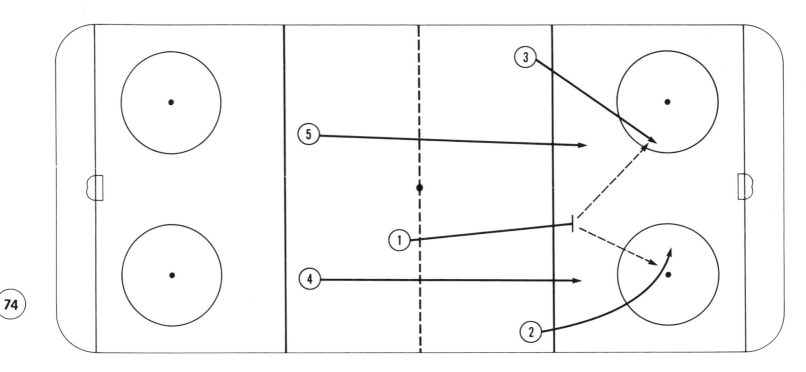

24. Occasionally a puckcarrier finds himself with the
opportunity to carry the puck into the offensive
zone because defencemen have back-skated deep
and wide. He then has the option to shoot, to pass to
one or the other of the wings breaking for the goal,
or to drop pass to the point-men who move up to
their positions.

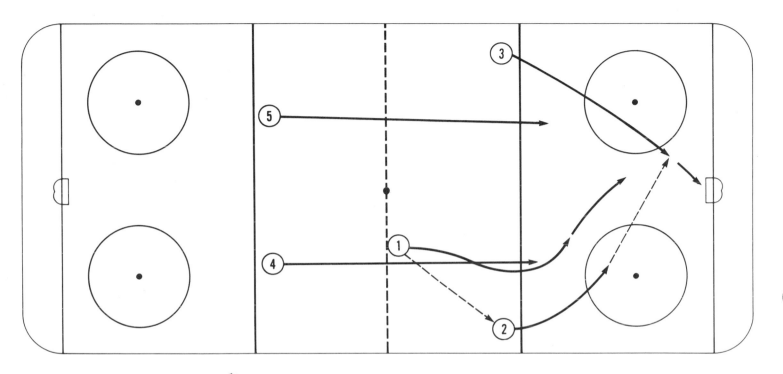

25. This is a simple variation of No. 1 and may be used if
a team is quite expert at passing and if the left wing,
in this example, is a little behind the play.

① passes to ② who begins to break for the slot, passes
to ③ who takes the shot.
① and ② follow-up for the rebound.

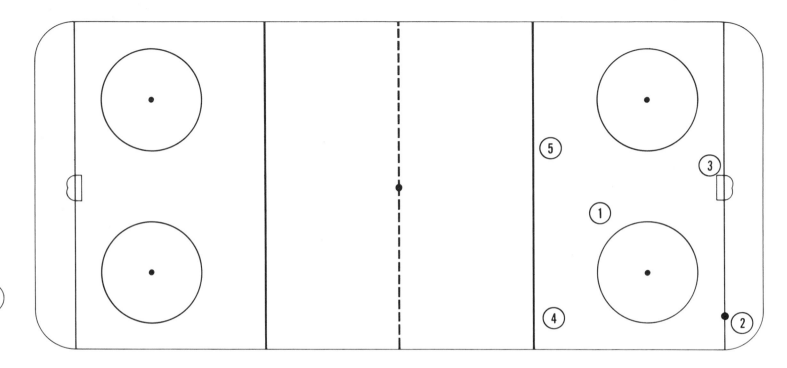

26. The Basic Offensive Pattern – puck in the corner

When the offensive team has possession of the puck in the opposition's corner, there *must* be ④ one player on the near point, ⑤ one player, slightly further inside and on the wide left point, ③ one player at the far post ready for deflections or passes behind the net, ① one player moving in the slot, and ② one player with the puck in the corner.

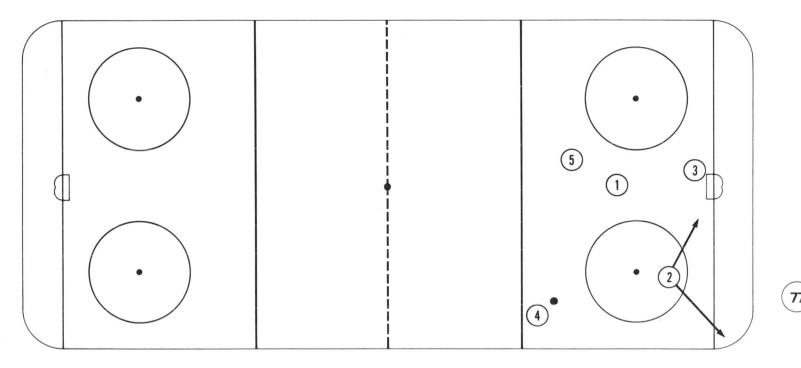

27. The Basic Offensive Pattern – puck at the point

When the offensive team has possession of the puck
at the point, it is essential to have ⑤ one player
playing the opposite point wide and slightly further
in, ③ one player on the far post for deflections, ① one
player roaming in the slot, and ② one player moving
from the corner to the near post and back to the
corner if the point man cannot get a clean shot at
goal.

THE IMPORTANCE OF "SWITCHING"

Modern hockey demands a tremendous amount of mobility on the part of all players. Coaches, players and fans who have watched and admired the play of defencemen like Bobby Orr of Boston, Tim Horton, formerly of Toronto, Serge Savard of Montreal, Carl Brewer of Toronto, Detroit and St. Louis must have noticed the number of times they have led offensive rushes or assumed positions as breaking wings. By the same token, players like Gordon Howe, Jean Beliveau, Yvan Cornoyer, Norm Ullman, Red Berenson, all forwards, have often taken up offensive point positions. It is to keep this flexibility in the attack that numbers, rather than letters, have been used in the preceding diagrams to describe positions.

The single essential concept is this: when a team begins its attack in its own zone, it must move out in either a 3-2 or a 4-1 alignment; when a team moves through the neutral zone, it must try to achieve a 2-1-2 alignment; and when a team has possession in the offensive zone, it must try to maintain the 2-1-2 alignment.

The large majority of goals are initiated at the points, and result directly from shots or from deflections, rebounds or caroms. The points *must always* be filled. Where it is impossible to get a shot away from the point, point players must understand that they have two major options, to pass back to the corner or to pass to the opposite point. The faster the passes are made, the more a team lets the puck "do its work", the greater are the chances of forcing the opposition out of the slot. And, when this happens, goals should be inevitable.

If a point player skates into the slot to shoot, his spot should be covered by the opposite point; and the latter's position should be filled by the slot man who drops straight back. This simple offensive rotation is illustrated in diagram No. 28.

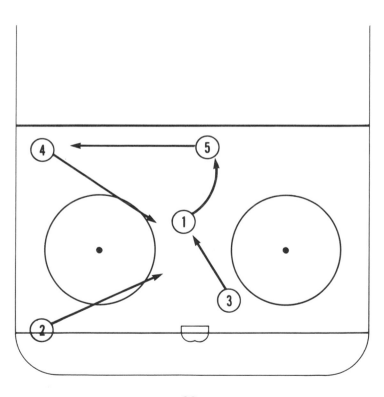

28.

PLAYING THE TWO ON ONE

The 2 on 1 offensive break is extremely common, particularly when an opposing pattern is broken up in the neutral zone. In these 2 on 1 situations, the puckcarrier and his teammate have three basic alternatives:

(a) The puckcarrier retains possession of the puck while his teammate attempts to draw the one defender away from the puck by manoeuvering to the outside.
(b) The puckcarrier draws the defender to him and, in the process of fading to the side, passes to his teammate.
(c) The puckcarrier drop passes the puck to his teammate and then serves as a screen while the latter completes the play.

In all instances, it is important that the puckcarrier attempt to line himself up with the one defender rather than allow the latter to assume a position between him and his teammate.

PLAYING THE ONE ON TWO

There is no good reason why a 1 on 2 attack should succeed since the first defender will check the man while the second picks up the loose puck. In these instances, and particularly when no assistance is in sight, the best single move is to take a shot on goal.

PLAYING THE ONE ON ONE

Whenever a player gets the opportunity to pick up the puck and "make a run" for the goal, he should look around to see who might be following up on the play and thus allow the 1 on 1 to be converted to a 2 on 1. It is a relatively easy matter for a defender to stop a 1 on 1 by playing the man rather than the puck. Thus, the puckcarrier must always be ready to shoot, utilizing as much as possible good head and shoulder faking in the hope that the defender will "go" with the fakes.

PLAYING THE THREE ON ONE

It is inexcusable to waste an opportunity that sees the offence with a two-man advantage over the defence. The puck must be carried into the offensive zone in the side alley and one of the three attackers *must* assume a trailing position which leads him to the slot. Because the defender will try to play a position from which he can cover the puckcarrier and the slot, a wide pass to the opposite wing breaking for the post can be successful. Regardless, an accurate shot, unhurried and well placed, is the key here.

Every face-off in the opposition's end of the ice can be considered as the start of an offensive play. Thus, the alignment assumed by offensive players is extremely important. In addition, and because it is easier to draw the puck backhand than forehand, coaches will often assign a left hand shot to take the face-off in the right corner and a right hand shot to take the face-off in the left corner. The face-off man has two major options: a shot on goal *or* a draw to the slot. It must be added, however, that the essential thing is to get the draw by using the most talented player in the face-off circle. A right-handed player in the right circle can shoot on goal or draw to the side boards; a left-handed player in the left circle can do likewise. Thus, four basic alignments should be practised, as follows:

80

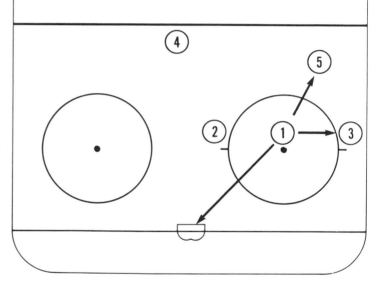

29. Face-off in the Left Corner with a Left-Handed Center

① – draws to left or back to left point, or shoots on goal.
② – checks and clears in front of net.
③ – gets puck or checks in left corner.
④ – lines up opposite right goal post
⑤ – plays in relatively close for back draw.

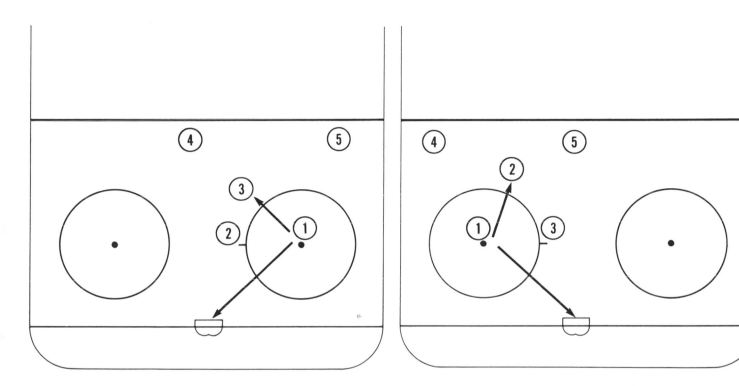

30. Face-off in the Left Corner with a Right-Handed Center

① – draws to slot or shoots on goal.
② – checks his man to allow ③ to shoot.
③ – assumes slot position and is ready to shoot.
④ – plays slightly wider to pick up passes through slot.
⑤ – plays deeper here.

31. Face-off in the Right Corner with a Left-Handed Center

the opposite to the situation outlined in No. 30.

81

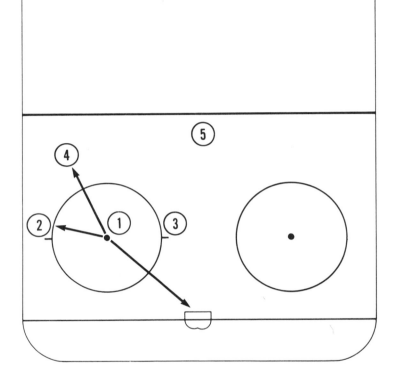

32. Face-off in the Right Corner with a Right-Handed Center

the opposite to the situation outlined in No. 29.

Thus, a complete offensive system involves a repertoire of patterns designed to:

(a) move the puck out of the defensive zone,
(b) move it quickly through the center alley of the neutral zone,
(c) carry it or shoot it into the attacking zone,
(d) move defenders out of the "slot",
(e) result in goals.

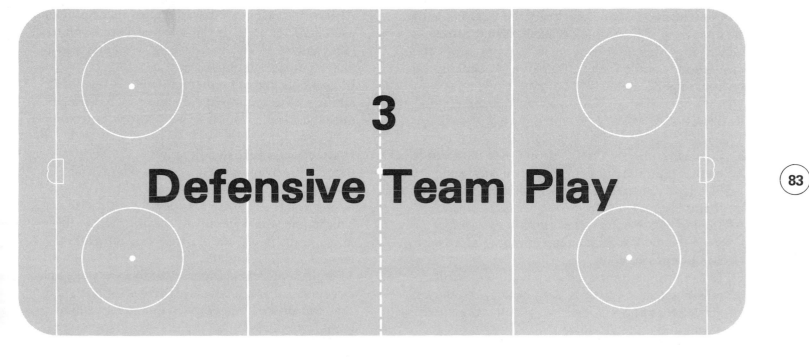

3
Defensive Team Play

INTRODUCTION

The object of a defensive system is to prevent the opposition from scoring goals by securing possession of the puck and moving instantly to the attack. Thus, any sound defensive system *must* begin the instant a team loses possession of the puck regardless of location on the ice. Vigorous forechecking in the opponent's defensive zone coupled with efficient backchecking are the keys to good defensive hockey.

A number of basic principles must be understood at the outset:

(a) Defensive players should always play the *man* (rather than the puck) in their own zone and in the offensive zone when the numerical strength of both teams is equal.

(b) In playing the man, it is essential to move him away from the puck so that a teammate can more easily achieve possession.

(c) In executing a check, players should take full advantage of the boards, the corners, and the net – three areas and/or obstacles which make checking easier and more effective.

(d) It is essential that checks be maintained long enough to prevent the checked player from re-entering the play, but not so long that needless interference penalties are applied.

(e) In the process of checking against the boards, it is important to "tie up" the opponent's stick and feet so that he is unable to execute a pass.

(f) Although when successful they look spectacular, the least important and most dangerous type of check is the hip check.

(g) Although less spectacular, the most successful and useful type of check is the one in which the checker faces square on his man, driving his shoulder at his check's chest and upper arms.

(h) In backchecking it is essential to cover the check all the way to one's goal area and to stay with him until the whistle sounds or possession of the puck is achieved.

(i) In situations where the offensive team enjoy a numerical advantage (e.g., 2 on 1, 3 on 1, and 3 on 2 breaks), defensive players should try to force the opposition to shoot from a spot outside the slot. This implies the necessity of playing neither the man nor the puck, but of protecting the area in front of the goaltender.

(j) Miscellaneous checking devices like the poke and sweep check are of considerably less importance than the ability to meet the man and move him from the puck.

The process of playing sound defensive hockey can be structured into a number of patterns which govern play in the defensive and the attacking zones.

DEFENSIVE PATTERNS

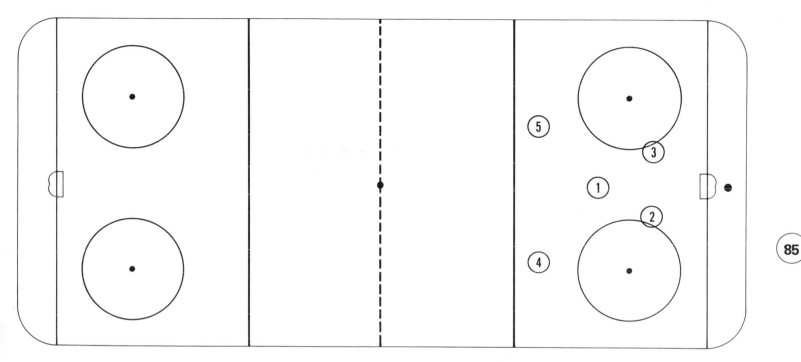

1. Puck in possession of opposition behind their own goal:

① – 20 feet from goal ready to follow up on check
② and ③ – 10 feet from goal ready to check puck-carrier
④ and ⑤ – well inside blue line.

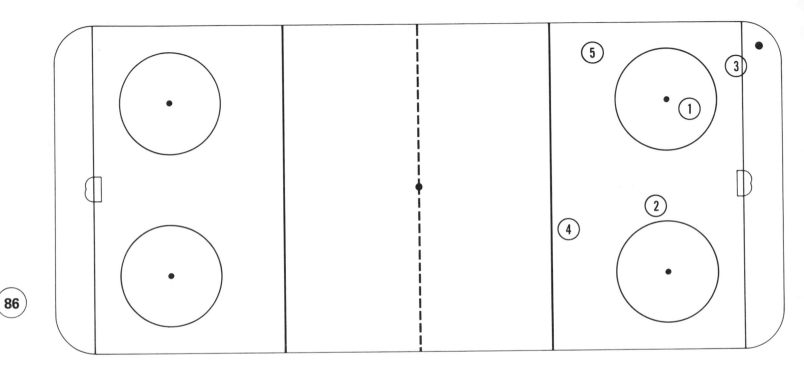

2. Puck in possession of opposition in defensive corner:

① – moves in to pick up the puck
② – moves from post to slot position
③ – plays the puckcarrier and moves him from the
     puck
④ – back on point
⑤ – well inside blue line to pick up possible pass.

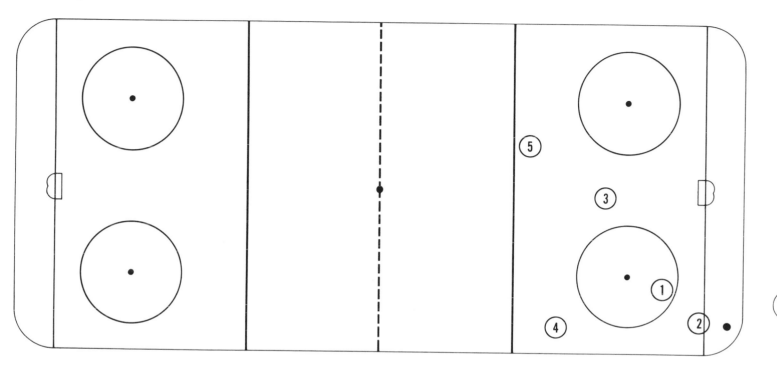

3. Puck in possession of opposition in opposite corner:

① – moves in to pick up puck
② – plays the puckcarrier
③ – moves to slot
④ – moves in from point for possible pass
⑤ – plays deep point.

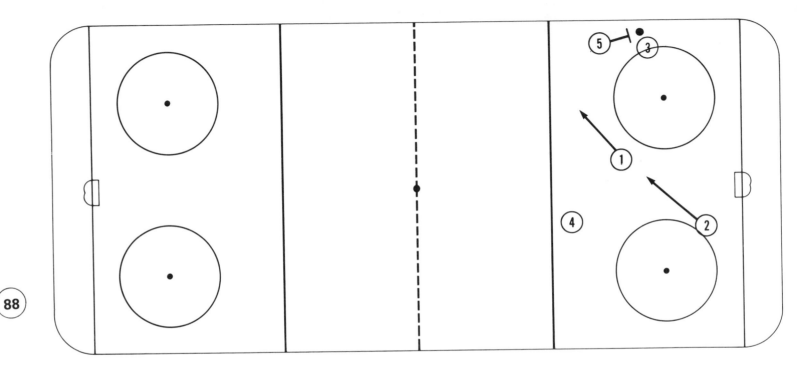

4. Puck in possession of opposition on boards near left point:

Where it is clear that there is no possibility of more than two opponents breaking out of their own end ahead of the nearest backchecker:

①- moves from slot to left point
②- moves from post to slot
③- moves in for the puck
④- retains right point
⑤- moves in to play the man.

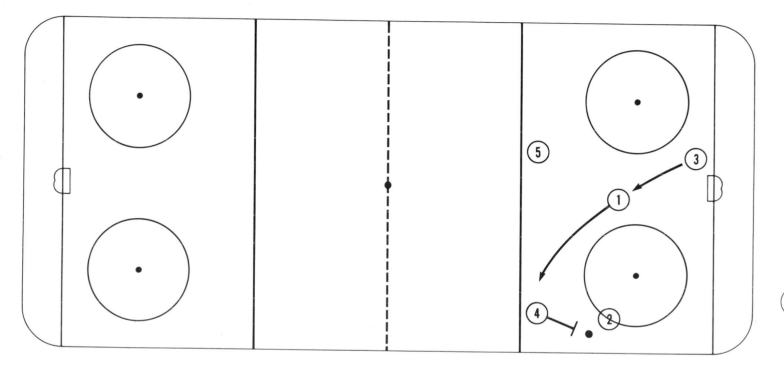

5. Puck in possession of opposition on boards near right point – same conditions prevail as in No. 4:

① – moves from slot to right point
② – moves in to secure the puck
③ – moves from post to slot
④ – moves in to play the man
⑤ – retains left point.

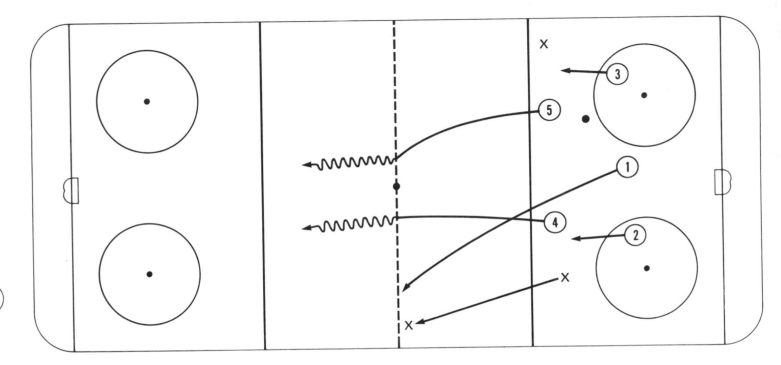

6. When the opponents have the puck in their end, are in the process of moving it up the ice and have more than two players ahead of the nearest backchecker, then:

① - presumably the shallowest checker picks up a wing
② and ③- hustle to get back and cover the offensive point players
④ and ⑤- skate to red line and turn, begin skating backwards.

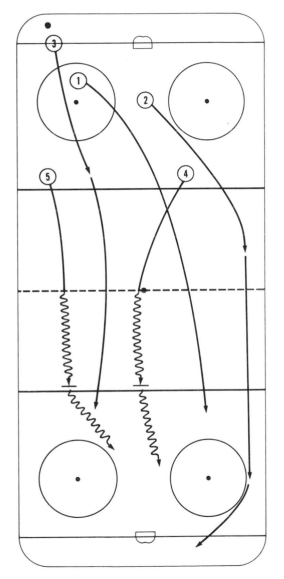

7. From a two-man forecheck in the corner to back-checking and defensive play in the defensive zone:

① – attempting to secure the puck
② – moves to cover the slot
③ – playing the man in the corner

① and ③ – scramble to get back to help out
② – covers an open wing as a backchecker
④ and ⑤ – skate to red line, turn, skate backwards to the blue line to make their play

① and ③ – cover the offensive points
② – takes his check all the way to the corner
④ and ⑤ – if unsuccessful in stopping the play at the blue line (e.g., 3 on 2, or 4 on 2), protect the slot.

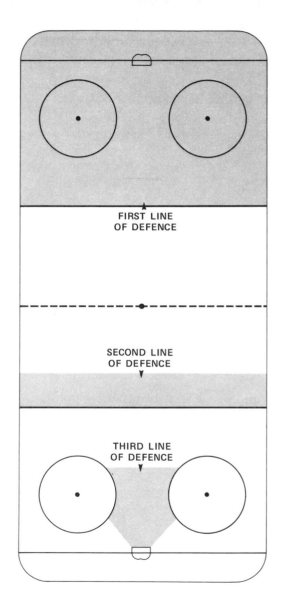

FIRST LINE
OF DEFENCE

SECOND LINE
OF DEFENCE

THIRD LINE
OF DEFENCE

8. It is important that defencemen understand that they should make their defensive play:

first in the attacking zone,
second at the defensive blue line, and
third in their own defensive zone.

One major error involves defencemen "backing" into their defensive zone instead of forcing off-sides at the defensive blue line.

THE TECHNIQUE OF FORECHECKING

Since most offensive patterns begin behind the goal, it is essential that forecheckers set themselves up so that they can force the puckcarrier to pass the puck. It is essential that they be warned *not* to chase a puck-carrier behind the goal, for to do so could result in their missing their check altogether and/or permitting the puckcarrier to make a successful pass. As soon as the puckcarrier begins his move from behind the goal, the checker should attempt to make contact either at the goal post or in the corner. The check must be executed under control; over-checking can result in the defensive team finding itself a man short.

As indicated earlier in this section, the object is to move the puckcarrier away from the puck so that the second forechecker can pick up the puck. If the first checker misses, then the second man should play the man while the first goes after the puck. Regardless of position, the nearest defender to the puckcarrier should play the man, the second nearest should go after the puck, the remaining players should rotate positions so that the points and the slot are *always* covered. In the process of lining up a check, the checker must anticipate where the puckcarrier will be at the point of contact and must meet him in such a way that his (the puckcarrier's) stick and feet are pinned against the boards or the net. By so doing, the checker eliminates any offensive threat from that player.

THE TECHNIQUE OF BACKCHECKING

Once it is clear that the offensive team is able to move the puck out of its own end, the defender nearest the offensive blue line must pick up a wing and backcheck him all the way to his own goal. It must be emphasized here that he *must* pick up an open wing and *not* the puckcarrier. In backchecking he should concentrate his attention on his check, not on the puck or the puck-carrier. It is his responsibility to prevent his check from scoring, and this he can best do if he aligns himself in such a position that his check cannot cut in front of or behind him. If he can stay close enough to his check, he will assist his defencemen immeasurably in that the combination of his closeness and their aggressive play at the defensive blue line will often force an off-side.

It is stressed that the first backchecker cover an open wing; this then allows the defencemen to concentrate on the puckcarrier and a second wing, reducing a 3 on 2 break to a 1 on 1. If the defencemen have the good fortune of seeing two backcheckers covering wings closely, then the offensive pattern is reduced to a 1 on 2, thus allowing one defenceman to take the man and the second to pick up the puck. In *no* instance should a backchecker ever drop his check to assist in covering the puckcarrier. Backcheckers who fail to do their job properly usually commit one of two mistakes: dropping their checks or paying too much attention to the puckcarrier and the puck.

CHECKING
IN FRONT OF YOUR GOAL

Defenders who find themselves responsible for checking opponents in front of their own goal need keep only three points in mind:

(a) maintain contact with the opponent (body or stick contact);
(b) maintain a position between the check and the goal;
(c) explode on your check the moment he drops his head to receive a pass or take a shot on goal.

There is a tendency for checkers to cross-check their opponents. This is not only a serious infraction of the rules, it is also poor hockey technique in that the whole object of checking is to gain possession of the puck, and in order to do this all players *must* keep the blades of the sticks on or near the ice. More passes or free pucks are missed by players who cross-check and high stick their checks; and more cheap penalties are incurred in this way. Coaches should stress the absolute rule that stick blades belong on the ice!

94

DEFENDING
AGAINST SPECIFIC PATTERNS

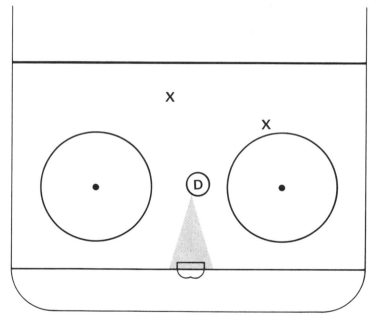

9. Defending against the 2 on 1 pattern:

Try to secure a position between the two attackers forcing the puckcarrier away from the slot. Do not over-commit yourself to either player but play the puckcarrier a *little* more closely than his teammate. Remember that the goaltender can assist by "covering" in part the open wing. The key is to force a shot from outside the slot.

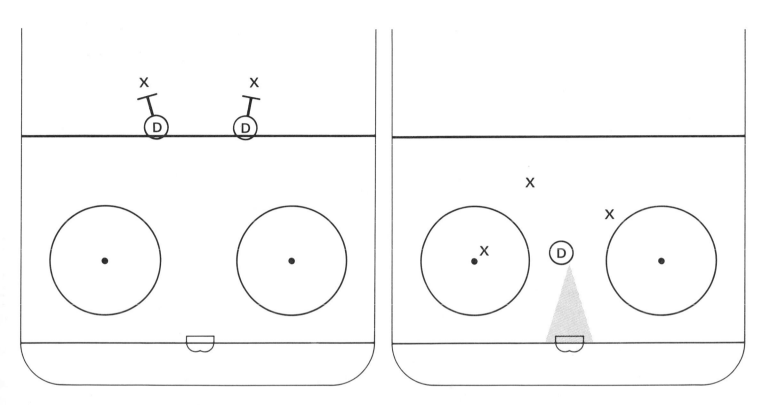

10. Defending against the 2 on 2 pattern:

This is a man-on-man situation; one defenceman covers the puckcarrier, the other covers the open wing. If each does his job, then, theoretically, the puckcarrier should be taken away from the puck and the open wing should be unable to pick up the loose puck. Care must be taken with respect to a possible trailer – if there is one, then the players must be ready to defend against a 3 on 2.

11. Defending against the 3 on 1 pattern:

It follows that any 3 on 1 break should result in a goal. The defender must do his best to force either a shot from outside the slot or a pass that is badly delivered or badly handled. Back in to the apex of the slot and attempt to "draw" the shot as early as possible.

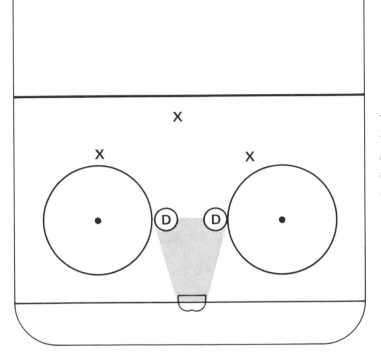

When face-offs are held in the defensive zone (both teams at full strength), then the defensive team must align itself in relation to the set-up adopted by the attacking team (cf. Part II – Offensive Face-Off Alignments). The important elements here are:

(a) to cover the man in the slot;
(b) to provide checkers at both points as quickly as possible;
(c) to tie up the opponent in front of the net in the event that a shot on goal is taken from the face-off;
(d) to be in position to go to the attack assuming possession of the puck is achieved.

12. Defending against the 3 on 2 pattern:

Defenders must cover the wide slot area and with the assistance of the goaltender convert this attack to a 1 on 1; that is, as soon as the shot is delivered, one defender takes one opponent, the second takes another, and the goaltender covers the puck and the third opponent.

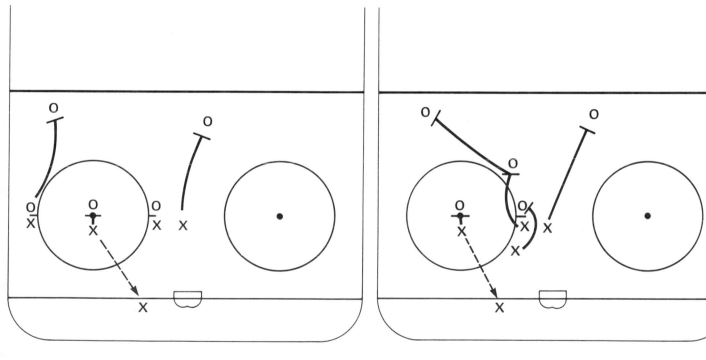

13. Attacking team with right hand shot taking the face-off in left corner (or left hand shot in right defensive corner).

14. Attacking team with left hand shot taking the face-off in left corner (or right hand shot in left defensive corner).

DEFENSIVE PLAY WHEN ONE MAN SHORT

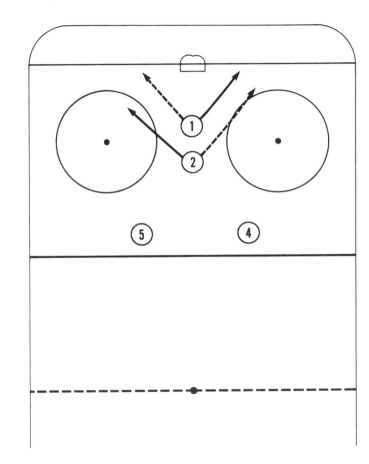

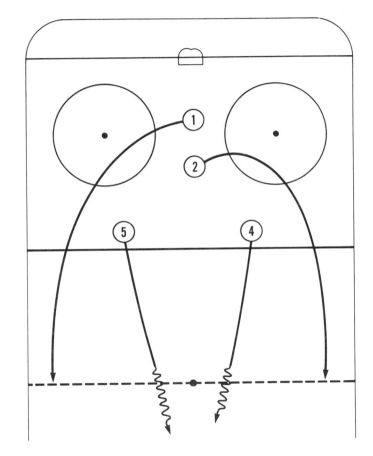

15. In the offensive zone:

- forecheckers ① and ② are "stacked" in front of goal
- defencemen ④ and ⑤ play points conservatively.

16. In the neutral zone:

- forecheckers ① and ② begin backchecking
- defencemen turn and skate to center ice line then begin skating backwards.

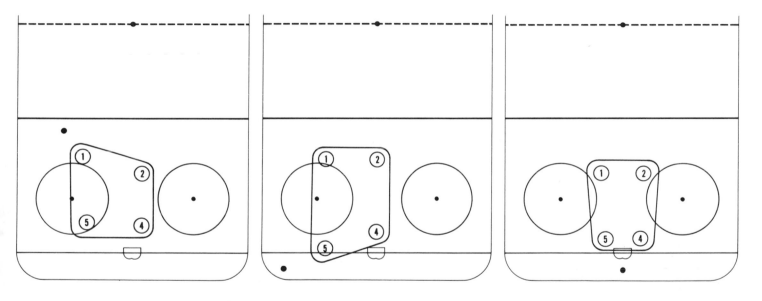

17. When the puck is at the point:

① – covers point
② – covers slot
④ and ⑤ – cover goal

18. When the puck is in the corner:

① – covers point
② – covers slot
④ – covers goal
⑤ – covers corner

19. When the puck is behind the goal:

① and ② – cover slot
④ and ⑤ – cover goal

DEFENSIVE PLAY WHEN TWO MEN SHORT

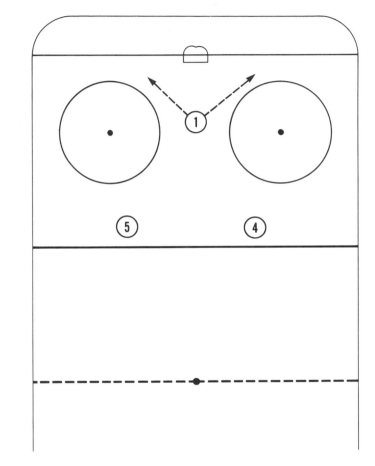

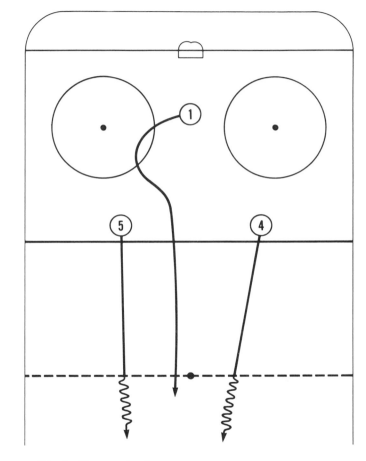

20. In the offensive zone:

① – forechecks in front of goal

④ and ⑤ – play points conservatively

21. In the neutral zone:

① – backchecks in center alley to force puck to the sides

④ and ⑤ – retreat to defensive blue line

In the defensive zone:

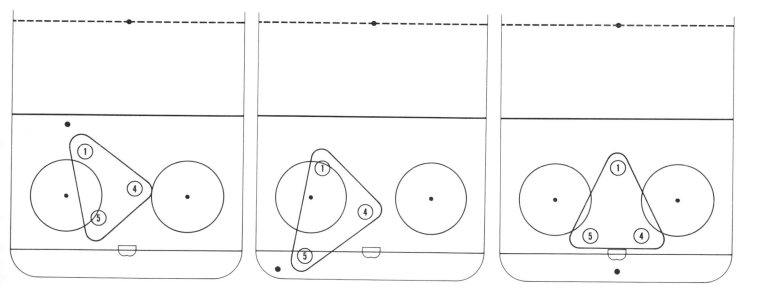

22. When the puck is at the point:

① – covers the point
④ – covers the slot
⑤ – covers the goal

23. When the puck is in the corner:

① – covers the point
④ – covers the slot
⑤ – covers the corner

24. When the puck is behind the goal:

① – covers the slot
④ and ⑤ – cover the goal

FACE-OFF ALIGNMENTS WHEN SHORT-HANDED

WHEN ONE MAN SHORT

WHEN TWO MEN SHORT

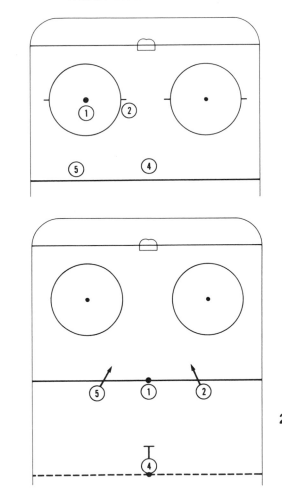

25. In The Attacking Zone

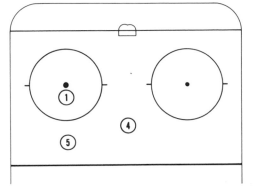

26. Outside The Offensive Blue Line

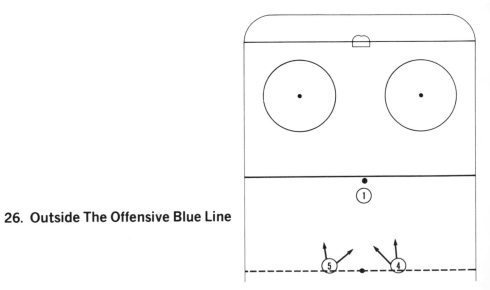

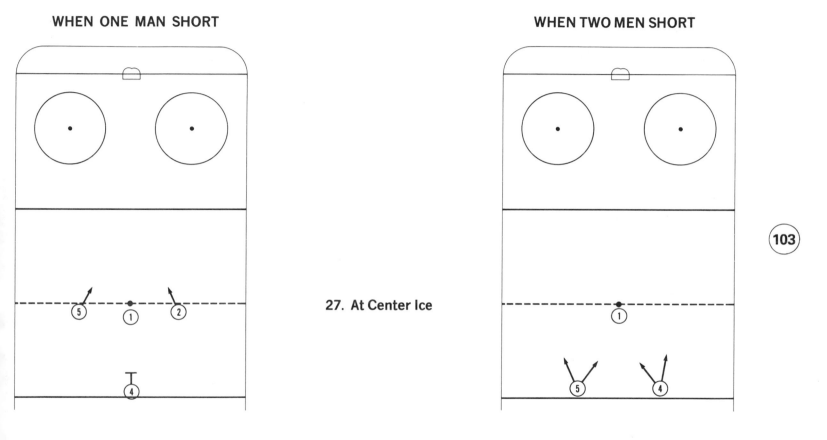

WHEN ONE MAN SHORT

WHEN TWO MEN SHORT

27. At Center Ice

103

WHEN ONE MAN SHORT

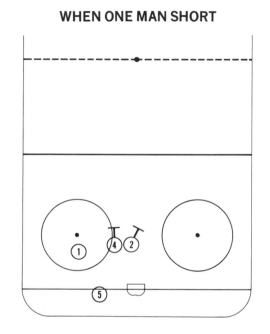

WHEN TWO MEN SHORT

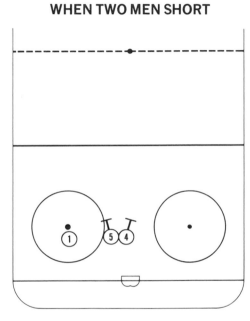

28. In The Defensive Zone

4

Coaching The Goaltenders

INTRODUCTION

The hockey goaltender is not unlike the baseball pitcher or the football quarterback in that a team's success or failure depends so much on the quality of his performance. And yet, despite this fact, hockey coaches spend less time on the average with their goaltenders than with any other players on the team! As one professional coach put it recently, "The one thing that worries me about my new coaching job is what to do with the goaltenders. I never played the spot. How can I help them? Will they listen to me?"

The key to coaching goaltenders is time – time to make positive suggestions, to concentrate on eliminating goaling weaknesses, to develop confidence, to get across the idea that goalers are expected to stop all or most shots delivered from outside the slot and to play the percentages on shots from within. Thus, coaches are urged to devote part of every practice to shooting and goaltending (cf. Part V).

GOALTENDING "STYLES"

For a number of years goalers were identifiable by their styles. There were "stand-up" goaltenders like Brimsek of Boston, and Bower of Toronto; there were deep-crouch goalers like Sawchuk of Detroit and Hall of Chicago and St. Louis; and there were the falling, smothering types of goalers like Worsley of New York, Montreal, and lately, Minnesota. But these styles were related more to body build and less to the nature of the game of hockey. And the nature of the game has changed as a result of the introduction and widespread use of the slap shot and the curved stick blade. Players are shooting from further out, harder, higher, faster than ever before. And as a concomitant to the long shot, more time and attention is being given to the fine art of deflecting and screening shots as mastered by Camille Henry of New York and Yvan Cournoyer of Montreal. This change has forced goalers to adopt a style that keeps them on their feet as much as possible to cover high shots from the point (and beyond) as well as flip shots from in close. In addition, it has forced goalers to play well out in front of the goal in order to reduce the size of the target. For a few years goalers used to move out as a threat developed and then start backing in to protect themselves from being "pulled" to one side or the other. Today it is generally agreed that shots from within the slot should be sure goals and that goaltenders should concentrate on getting out front, staying there, and preventing goals from areas outside of the slot. A few goalers (and the latest and possibly greatest master of this technique is Ken Dryden of Montreal) have developed a real facility for poke-checking – stealing the puck off a potential scorer's stick if he happens to cruise in too close to the goal. Thus, the combination of (a) staying up on the feet, (b) moving well out in front to reduce angle and net opening, and (c) poke-checking players who carry the puck well into the slot constitutes the most acceptable and successful style.

THE DECREASING IMPORTANCE OF THE HANDS

Most books on hockey suggest that the most important ingredient of good goaltending is the ability to use one's hands to stop pucks. This was true for many years but is considerably less so today. Many goaltenders (Jacques Plante of Toronto is an example) concentrate on holding the catching hand and arm low and against the pads to increase the width of the leg guards. The fact that goalers now concentrate on staying on their feet (rather than falling to smother shots) has reduced significantly the importance of the hands as defensive tools. The legs, feet, skate blades and stick are the more important puck-stopping devices. This is not intended to imply that goaltenders should forget about developing fast and sure hands; rather, it is intended to suggest that, in the process of selecting goalers, less emphasis should be placed on hand dexterity and more on other defensive skills.

THE ESSENTIALS OF GOOD GOALTENDING

It is obvious that good goaltenders should possess a liberal amount of courage and should, as well, have fast reflexes. But there are other ingredients including the following:

(A) SKATING ABILITY

Former Toronto coach, Howie Meeker, has often said that the goaltender should be the best skater on the team. Who else, he contends, has to stop and start so often, skate forwards and backwards, side to side, drop to his knees, and scramble back to his feet, skate around the net to stop pucks that skirt the boards, and dash forward to pick up loose pucks or block high clearing shots? His point is well made – goalers must be superb skaters and skating must be one of the major conditioning and training elements in their development.

(B) STICK CONTROL

Reference has already been made to the use of the stick as a poke-checking defensive tool. But it should also be added that a goaltender must learn to keep the blade of his stick on the ice and about ten to twelve inches in front of his skates. Far too many young goaltenders hold the stick at a point too low on the shaft. Thus, when they straighten up the stick automatically rises from the ice. And too many hold the blade against their skate toes, thus providing rebounds (because the stick blade is rigid) or losing the puck from view since it is almost impossible to see a puck at one's feet if wearing a protective mask. It is important that the coach mark a spot on the shaft where the stick should be held for best results and that a large knob of tape be placed on the shaft end so that the goaler can "shoot" his stick out to poke-check an opponent without losing possession of this all-important tool.

(C) PLAYING THE ANGLES

The good goaltender is one who is thoroughly familiar with the best position to assume to reduce the amount of open net insofar as any and every location on the ice is concerned. The further out front he plays, the less direct contact he has with the posts, thus the more difficult it is to develop a sense of orientation vis-à-vis the goal. The circular crease used in some levels of amateur hockey is a great assistance in this regard; the rectangular crease poses greater orientation problems. Some coaches like to place marks on the ice, small V's, to assist the goaler in developing a greater sense of location awareness; others insist that goalers assume positions in relation to the set-up of lighting fixtures or by taking sights on the opposite goal some 190 feet away. But it is clear that goalers should always start from a position that provides direct contact with the goal and move out from there. This gives them an initial "fix" that will last through that one play sequence. All goalers should determine the best location to stop shots from the two points, the front of the slot and from the two corner face-off spots – these are five locations from which shots are frequently delivered.

(D) MASTERING THE "HINGE" PRINCIPLE

When the puck is in the defensive corners, behind the goal or in the area between the goal and the corners, the goaltender should assume a position "on" the post nearer the puck. The outside of his foot should be held firmly against the post, with the leg pad overlapping the post for maximum security. As the puck moves to the opposite corner, he is in a perfect position to drive across the goal mouth, using the post as a fixed starting block. When located "on" the post he should operate in a manner similar to a hinged door so that he is always facing (as much as possible) the puck. It is important to train the goaler to use his stick effectively in this position since difficulty is sometimes experienced through getting the stick tangled in the netting.

The goaltender who can master these four ingredients: superb skating ability, excellent stick control, mastery at playing the angles, and operating as a hinged door on the posts, will meet with the greatest amount of success. It must be stressed that these abilities can only be developed through constant directed practice. And the time so spent will surely prove to be the greatest investment a coach can make.

SOME SPECIFIC SUGGESTIONS FOR GOALTENDERS

1. Keep a catalogue of your mistakes, shots that you missed, where they came from, what move you made or didn't make.

2. Stand up as much as possible; this way you'll cover more of the net.

3. Concentrate on the puck no matter where it is on the ice – and that includes the far end of the ice.

4. Talk to your teammates; give them specific directions or guidance.

5. Cut off pucks that hit or skirt around the end boards and set them up for your teammates. Don't leave them against the bottom of the boards; they are too hard to get under control; set them up from 6 to 12 inches from the boards.

6. Always direct your rebound or tosses away from the flow of the traffic, that is, if a shot came from your left side, steer the rebound or toss to the left since the shooter will normally follow in on his shot and thus move to your right.

7. Don't cause useless whistles; try to get the puck off to the corner or up to an open player, particularly when the opposition is forechecking.

8. Be on the lookout for players who drop their heads and eyes before shooting; the moment they look down, explode out to block the shot.

9. Try to eliminate rebounds by smothering shots with your catching glove; you can avoid rebounds from your stick by keeping it out in front of your feet, and not up against the toes of the boots and blades.

10. Once you move out, don't move back; rather concentrate on holding your ground and forcing the shooter to pick the one or two small open spots.

11. Remember that you go down and slide *only* as a last desperate move because once you are down you are usually out of the play in the event of a rebound.

12. Use your stick as a major defensive weapon; "shoot" it out at an opponent's stick to deflect the puck.

13. When your vision is blocked, crouch lower to keep your eye on the puck.

14. Remember to concentrate on the puck and not the man insofar as ice position is concerned. A right hand shot will shoot the puck from a location about four feet to your left as he pulls the puck back and to the side prior to the release.

15. Always survey the area in front of your goal before each period looking for bumps, cracks in the ice, etc. Keep the area clear and smooth so that you won't be caught by unfortunate bounces.

16. Warm-up well before the game; have your teammates keep their shots low and on target; the purpose of the exercise is to get you ready and confident.

17. Never get sloppy in your puckhandling in practice, in warm-ups, or in a game. It is too easy to develop bad habits.

18. In 2 on 1 situations, take the open man yourself by anticipating his move in the event of a pass.

CHARTING GOALTENDING SUCCESS AND FAILURE

It has already been stated that goalers should be expected to stop the large majority of shots from locations outside the slot and to play the percentages (position, stick-checking, cutting off angles) on shots from within the slot.

The goaler's ability and consistency can, therefore, be assessed at least in part by charting the locations from which shots are directed at his goal, and recording those which he stops and those which elude him. It is sufficient to identify six areas as outlined below:

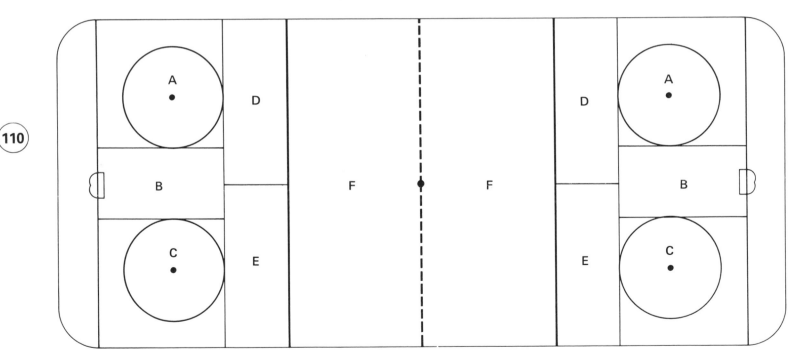

If the manager were instructed to insert an "x" on the appropriate spot from which a shot on goal is made and to circle the "x" if the goal is scored, then it becomes a rather simple matter to identify goaltending weaknesses and strengths, and then to take remedial action.

If a large number of goals are scored from areas "A" and/or "C" then the coach should re-teach the hinge principle; he might also review the skill of blocking shots with the stick blade and skate on the long side.

If a large number of goals are scored from areas "D" and "E" then it will be necessary for the coach to drill his goaltender on:
- moving out to meet shots from the point,
- getting low and rising with the shot,
- getting his body behind all long shots,
- smothering rebounds.

If a number of goals are scored from area "F" then the coach must drill his goaler on:
- concentrating on the puck when it is outside his defensive zone,
- moving out to meet the shot, particularly bouncing shots.

Hopefully goaltenders will stop their fair share of shots from within the slot. The better-than-average goaler is the one who stays on his feet, forces the opposition to make the first move, and exhibits excellent control of his stick as a blocking and checking implement.

The goalers who should be chosen from the masses are those, then, who are most consistently successful in stopping shots from areas "A", "C", "D", "E", and "F".

5

Coaching and Teaching Hockey

INTRODUCTION

There are at least four ingredients that are required if hockey (or, for that matter, any athletic activity) is to be properly taught and or coached:

A. Planning
B. Communication
C. Analysis, correction
D. Motivation

It is assumed that the teacher or coach has, as a preliminary to these, adequate knowledge and understanding of the sport of hockey, its fundamental and team techniques.

PLANNING FOR TEACHING AND COACHING

There are two types of plans which *must* be developed by the teacher or coach if his program is to be well presented: the master or seasonal or unit plan *and* the individual lesson or practice plan.

The master or seasonal plan is a general outline of the course or the season and should include at least the following:

(a) the starting and ending dates of the instructional unit or competitive season;
(b) the material or skill content to be taught/coached;
(c) the critical path to be followed insofar as instructional testing or competitive game dates are concerned.

(It is also desirable to include in the master plan a list of the objectives to be achieved, a bibliography and a list of equipment required.) The master or seasonal plan should provide the teacher or coach with a blueprint to follow insofar as the preparation of individual lesson or practice plans are concerned as well as a ready reference summary of all that must be done in advance of testing or schedule commitments during the unit or season. In these respects then it is the more important plan and deserves the instructor's time and attention in its preparation.

The following are sample seasonal and unit master plans in outline form:

A SEASONAL PLAN FOR A MINOR OR SCHOOL HOCKEY TEAM

TEAM: **LEVEL:**

Dates: 1st team meeting –

           1st conditioning session –

           1st ice session –

           last day of season –

SCHEDULE OF GAMES:

     (a) November

     (b) December

     (c) January

     (d) February

     (e) March

PRACTICE-GAME SCHEDULE:

   Practices: Monday, Tuesday, Thursday – from _____ to _____

   Games: Wednesdays at _____; Fridays at _____

                  (occasional games on Saturdays – cf. schedule)

GENERAL PLAN OF OPERATION:

     (a) reduction of candidates to _____ by _____

     (b) reduction of candidates to _____ by _____

     (c) final cuts by _____

     (d) inter-squad game No. 1 – _____

     (e) inter-squad game No. 2 – _____

TEAM PERSONNEL:

   Coach –

   Assistant –

   Manager –

   Assistant –

   Physician –

   Alternate –

   Arena Manager –

EARLY SEASON CRITICAL PATH:

Conditioning and Chalk Board
— Start skating–puckhandling
— Start passing
— Start shooting
— Start forechecking
— Inter-squad Game No. 1
— Start backchecking
— Start power play and corner face-offs
— Start penalty killing
— Inter-squad Game No. 2
— Start changing on fly
— Start rebounding
— Start two men short
— Exhibition Game
— Regular Season

A UNIT PLAN FOR A SECONDARY SCHOOL INSTRUCTIONAL UNIT IN HOCKEY

UNIT: *Hockey*

GRADE LEVEL: *Junior High Boys*
NO. OF PERIODS: *18*

OBJECTIVES:

This unit is designed to –
(a) provide instruction in the four essential hockey fundamentals
(b) assist in preparing students for intramural, inter-school and community leagues and teams
(c) increase the skill level of the participants
(d) contribute to the students' overall fitness development.

STARTING DATE OF UNIT: *Nov. 1*   **ENDING DATE OF UNIT:** *Dec. 15*

CRITICAL DATES:

(a) Lesson 1 – overview, pre-tests on skating, puckhandling
(b) Lesson 8 – progress tests on skating, puckhandling, passing
(c) Lesson 17 – final tests on all skills
(d) Lesson 18 – summary

BASIC REFERENCES:

(a) *Coach's Manual – Hockey*, (Ottawa: Information Canada, 1965).
(b) "The World's Fastest Game" – films on fundamentals, (London, Ontario: Labatt Co.)

SKILL CONTENT	Wk. 1			Wk. 2			Wk. 3			Wk. 4			Wk. 5			Wk. 6		
	1	2	3	4	5	6	7	8	9	10	11	12	13	14	15	16	17	18
Warm-up																		
Skating – Forward																		
Backward																		
Stopping																		
Circles																		
Fwd. to bkwd.																		
Bkwd. to fwd.																		
Side-stepping																		
Puckhandling – Stationary																		
Moving																		
In pairs																		
With skates																		
Passing – Stationary																		
–forehand																		
–backhand																		
Moving																		
–forehand																		
–backhand																		
Flip passes																		
Receiving passes																		
–forehand																		
–backhand																		
Shooting – Wrist																		
Snap																		
Slap																		
Rebounding																		
Checking																		

Pre-tests and Overview

Progress Tests – skating, puckhandling, passing

Testing – skating, puckhandling, passing, shooting, checking

The individual lesson or practice plan is a precise outline of what the teacher or coach intends to cover in a specific class or practice period. It is *not* recommended that these be completed in toto in advance for to do so would imply that the students or players would progress at pre-determined rates, and that is hardly (if ever) the case. Each practice or class should be prepared in the light of what was accomplished in the previous session and in the light of problems which have arisen, weaknesses which have been uncovered, and gaps which need to be filled. In preparing these plans reference must be made to the skill content checklist in order to ensure appropriate emphasis.

The following are *sample lesson or practice plans* in outline form:

A LESSON PLAN
FOR A SECONDARY SCHOOL PHYSICAL EDUCATION CLASS IN HOCKEY

UNIT: *Hockey* **GRADE LEVEL:** *Junior High Boys* **LESSON NO.** _____

Objectives of the lesson:	
Warm-up activities:	Time:
Review of previous class:	Time:
Skills to be taught: Drills to be used:	Time:
Practice of skills:	Time:
Conditioning activities:	Time:
Comments:	

A PRACTICE PLAN FOR A MINOR OR SCHOOL HOCKEY TEAM

TEAM: LEVEL: PRACTICE NO. _____   DATE:

ITEM	DRILLS			TIME
Warm-up				
Skating – Passing – Puckhandling				
Area No. 1				
Shooting and goaltending				
Area No. 2				
Controlled scrimmage				
Conditioning				
Individual instruction: Names:				
Comments:				

Note: It is considered essential to work on conditioning, skating, puckhandling, passing, shooting, and goaltending in every practice session. The materials covered under "Area No. 1" and "Area No. 2" should be those items which cannot or need not be practised in every session (cf. Skill Content Checklist).

SKILL CONTENT CHECKLIST

SKILL CHECKLIST	DATES PRACTISED			
Skating: – starts and stops, forward – starts and stops, backward – backward to forward – forward to backward – side-stepping – hairpin turns				
Puckhandling and Passing: – 2 on 0 – 2 on 1 – 3 on 1 – 3 on 2 – 2 on 2 – 1 on 0 – 1 on 1 – 5 on 2 – 5 on 3 – 5 on 4				
Shooting: – wrist – snap – slap – deflections – from face-offs – long flip shots – screening				
Checking: – forechecking – backchecking – checking at points – checking at defensive blue – checking in defensive corners – in front of own goal – in front of offensive goal – cutting off behind goal – at face-offs				

SKILL CHECKLIST *cont'd*

	DATES PRACTISED
Offensive system:	
– coming out of own end	
– neutral zone	
– offensive zone	
– offensive face-offs	
– power play	
Defensive system:	
– in their zone	
– in neutral zone	
– in defensive zone	
– face-offs	
Playing with advantage:	
– one man advantage	
– two men advantage	
Playing short-handed:	
– one man short	
– two men short	
Changing on the fly	
Playing with 6 attackers	
Playing against 6 attackers	
Pre-game warm-up	
Equipment care	
Special assistance:	
– goaltenders	
– defencemen	
– centers	
– wings	
– penalty killers	
– point personnel	
– weak skaters	
– weak checkers	
– weak shooters	
– weak passers	
Chalkboard Drills	

A SAMPLE PRACTICE PLAN FOR A MINOR OR SCHOOL TEAM

TEAM _____   PRACTICE NO. _____   DATE _____

PRACTICE	TIME
1. Warm-up – a) two easy laps of rink forward, one backward, reverse direction, two forward and one backward b) across and back – leg drags, stretches etc.	3 min.
2. Skating – passing – puckhandling – a) 3 on 2 working from both ends alternately b) 5 vs. 2 power play passing in each end – red and green lines – west end + def. pairs 1 and 3 – blue and white lines – east end + def. pairs 2 and 4	20 min.
3. Special area No. 1 – Coming out of own end – starting with puck behind net in defensive position a) west end – reds vs. whites b) east end – greens vs. blues	10 min.
4. Shooting – goaltending – west end – point shots and deflections east end – rebounding drill center ice – flip shot practice	10 min.
5. Special area No. 2 – changing on the fly reds and whites vs. blues and greens – full strength	6 min.
6. Controlled scrimmage – emphasizing forechecking reds and whites vs. blues and greens	10 min.
7. Conditioning – a) races by positions, 1 length – repeat 3 times b) pushing – pulling drills, using widths – 6 times; 2 fast laps	6 min.
Individual instruction with: centers on taking face-offs – Smith R., Jones H., Brown W.	
Comments –	

121

COMMUNICATION

Important though good planning is, it can only be as successful as the extent to which the teacher or coach "reaches" his athletes. The processes of communication add a personal, human dimension to comprehensive planning.

There are at least seven situations in which good coach-player or teacher-student communication is essential.

(I) PRE-SEASON COMMUNICATION

Although boys have a natural interest in sport participation, it must be acknowledged that a large number of activities and promoters are competing for their time and attention. Winter activities like skiing, curling, basketball, volleyball, wrestling and gymnastics are appealing, and quite legitimately so. Thus, it behooves the hockey coach to establish early communication with potential candidates, and, in the process, to outline:

- possible schedules of practices and games
- pre-season training procedures
- equipment, uniform and travel advantages
- the guiding philosophy that will prevail
- the nature and intensity of competition
- the availability of opportunities to "make the team"
- the system to be used offensively and defensively.

When boys begin to "think" hockey early and when they get involved in the process of conditioning them-selves for those early season practices, when they begin to talk about hockey and their own personal aspirations for the coming season, then a sense of keen anticipation is developed.

This form of communication can be accomplished through press releases, letters to candidates, the circulation of training schedules, publication of game schedules, in-school or community displays, pre-season get-togethers that feature hockey films and discussions, etc.

(II) LECTURE ROOM COMMUNICATION

Although hockey skills can best be learned on the ice, it is essential that candidates and players have a thorough understanding of the "how" and the "why" as well as the "what" of the game. Because of the high cost of ice time, coaches and teachers should plan to use lecture-discussion sessions throughout the season. These sessions can be devoted to such items as:

- an overview of the offensive system
- an overview of the defensive system
- game film or commercial film analysis
- problem-solving sessions
- discussion on strategy
- analysis of errors committed in the previous game
- instruction in drills to be employed in the next practice
- consideration of training, medical and managerial problems.

The use of chalkboards, magnetic boards, films, still pictures, loops, diagrams and live demonstrations is advocated. Many coaches who find that they just cannot get adequate ice time often supplement their allotment with lecture-discussion-practise sessions in school or community gymnasia or recreation halls, utilizing activities like floor hockey and soccer as teaching-training media.

(III) LOCKER ROOM COMMUNICATION

There is probably no greater waste in hockey than the time devoted to detailed explanations on the ice during a practice. The competent coach makes certain that he reviews his practice in the locker room while the players are "suiting-up". If new drills are to be used, they should be explained in detail here. The twenty or thirty minutes consumed in dressing for a practice can be used as another opportunity for coach-player or teacher-student communication.

(IV) ON-ICE COMMUNICATION

Because hockey arena acoustics are usually poor, the instructor has to think through the best techniques and formations to be employed when brief explanations and corrections are made on the ice. One often sees a coach standing in the center of a circle of players, a position where he is able to see only half his group at any one time and be heard by even fewer. Again, it is not uncommon to see a coach at one end of the ice "barking" instructions to players lined up at the other

end. It's hard on the voice; it's almost always unsuccessful; and it leads to confusion and irritation. These are the best positions: facing your group which is lined up near a players' bench, facing your forwards who are set up in lines at one end of the ice, giving explanations just prior to a corner face-off where all can see, be seen and hear. By far the most important and successful type of communication on the ice is that which involves the coach or teacher and one player; mass explanations should be reserved for the locker room or the lecture room.

(V) PRE-GAME, BETWEEN-PERIOD AND POST-GAME COMMUNICATION

Tension is a part of sport competition, and so is success and elation, failure and discouragement. The job of the coach as a communicator before, during and after games, is to try to reduce or harness this tension and to put success and failure in proper perspective. One win never makes a season and one loss hardly ever destroys a season. Thus, the coach's role is to bring a calm and a sense of confidence to his locker room, to clearly spell out alignments, starting assignments, basic strategy. In addition, between periods, it is his job to provide an opportunity for his players to review the previous twenty minutes of play, to understand what the opposition was doing that was successful and what must be done to counteract it, to reassure his goaltender and those who may have committed major or costly errors. Finally, when the game is over, it is his job to leave his players with the feeling that hockey is a game and that, win or lose, the main objective of the next practice will be to improve where improvement is required and to consolidate where success was experienced. When a team plays badly, it is neither sound nor appropriate to launch into a vehement soliloquy immediately following the game. The critique must combine analysis with prescription or direction, and this type of a presentation takes time to prepare.

(VI) COMMUNICATION ON THE BENCH

Far too many hockey coaches concentrate exclusively on the game and on the play of their own players. They seem to be completely involved in making line changes and maintaining bench discipline. The job of the bench coach is to analyze the opponents' strengths and weaknesses, to identify goaltending weaknesses, to dissect their system and to make adjustments in his own team's style of play. It is true that, as soon as a line change is made, the coach should inform his players with respect to the next change (assuming no penalty is called). He should also discreetly make suggestions to those who have just left the ice. But, more important, he should be indicating to *individuals* what they might do to meet with success when next they take their turn. For example, the opposing goaltender may appear "shaky" on long rising shots from the point. In this instance he should so inform his point players and, at the same time, tell his deflection specialists to back away from the posts a little more than usual so that they might create better screens of these shots. He may discover that opposing players over-commit themselves in the offensive zone, thus making themselves vulnerable to fast-breaking plays. This may require telling the wings to come back into their own end only as deep as the hash mark on the face-off circle rather than all the way to the goal line. This type of communication is positive, meaningful and is such that players will soon realize that the coach is much more than a line-changer.

(VII) POST-SEASON COMMUNICATION

The coach has a responsibility to his association, his management, his sponsors and his players to bring each season to a happy and enthusiastic end. This implies the need for one or more post-season summary, conclusion and evaluation sessions. Feedback is important if improvement is to result. The manager requires an opportunity to collect uniforms and equipment. The players want the opportunity to express their gratitude to those who made the season possible. Failure to conduct post mortems may result in the perpetuation of error.

ANALYSIS AND CORRECTION

Even the casual observer of sport realizes that most games or meets are lost because of mistakes committed rather than won as the result of superb play. For example, every time a tennis player commits a service double fault, he loses a point; his opponent did absolutely nothing to win the point. The same thing applies to hockey. Most goals result from errors, errors of skill, of judgment, of execution, of position. It follows, therefore, that all or most other things being equal, the team which makes the fewer number of mistakes will invariably win. Thus, the coach has the task of analyzing individual player and team performance, identifying basic common and individual errors and prescribing, directing, exhorting and drilling his players to the point that they commit these errors less frequently.

In order to do this the coach or teacher must *first* understand the correct way of performing a skill or pattern; *second*, communicate this correct way to his players or students; *third*, provide them with the opportunity to perfect the skill or pattern, and *fourth*, help them to understand what they are doing incorrectly and why they are doing so. Trite exhortations like "skate faster", "try harder", "do it right" and so forth, are utterly useless. For example, if a player frequently loses passes off his stick, he has to understand that the target he presents must be at right angles to the direction of the pass. Again, if a point player often shoots into the pads of a defender who then proceeds to break down ice, he has to understand the importance of looking at the goal when he shoots (and that takes considerable puckhandling practice) and he must also understand that he has at least two other options: to pass the puck to the offensive corner or across to his fellow point-man. If a goaltender "blows" a number of high floating shots from center ice, he has to understand the reasons for moving out of

his crease to meet the puck, when and how far he should move, and must have the opportunity to practice this skill often.

Thus, there are five steps which should be followed in the process of correcting error and eliminating mistakes:

(i)   proper teaching of the technique
(ii) adequate practice of the technique
(iii) careful analysis of the skill execution
(iv) a thorough understanding of the reasons for failure
(v)   reasonable and practical suggestions for improvement.

Because skill errors are individual matters, correction can best be done on a one-to-one basis involving the coach or teacher and the player. And, because skill errors are often habitual, great patience is required while the player undoes the previous skill learning as a preliminary to the adoption of a new and more successful pattern.

One of the heresies in hockey coaching is the amount of practice time devoted to scrimmage or inter-squad games. Youngsters love to play and to compete and so some scrimmage is essential. But players who commit basic skill errors and who are in the process of trying to adopt new patterns invariably return to erroneous patterns when their attention is directed completely to playing the game. The net result is that they reconfirm their errors or, as one coach put it recently, "they get better at doing things wrong" through uncontrolled scrimmage.

Players, and particularly young players, can only

cope with one or two skill patterns at a time. They must be free to concentrate on a specific task. The more specific and meaningful the task, the greater will be the learning rate and the retention rate.

Finally, the better the rapport between coach or teacher and player, and the greater the confidence the player has in the abilities and judgment of his instructor, the more successful will be the learning-coaching-performance process.

MOTIVATION

The intrinsically motivated hockey player is one who wants and needs success for its own sake. He loves the game, he literally lives for practices, games, drills, scrimmages. He is proud of himself, his performance, his improvement, his participation. He is, in short, a very unusual person. But intrinsically motivated hockey players do exist and are a treat to have on one's team.

The extrinsically motivated hockey player is one who needs to be encouraged, supported, driven and inspired by outside forces – teammates, crowds, publicity, awards, trips, the thrill of wearing the team jersey, the personality of the coach and so forth.

The first type is self-motivated, and got that way, in part at least, through a pleasant and encouraging home environment, a pre-disposition to sport and competition and through a desire to emulate an admired player or coach. The second type requires some assistance in

"getting up" for games, in persisting in practice, and in maintaining enthusiasm. The coach's and teacher's role is to bring to bear all the sound devices that can reasonably, economically and legitimately be employed to make hockey participation a thoroughly satisfying experience. These include, among many others:

- good coaching, competent leadership
- desirable environment, rink, locker room
- adequate and challenging but reasonable schedule
- well-planned practices
- adequate publicity and public interest
- good and attractice protective equipment and uniforms
- pleasant relationships with teammates
- a fair chance to make the team
- a fair share of success
- a sound rapport with coach, manager, promoter, administrator
- the opportunity to maintain dignity and self-respect
- the expectation to play if selected for the team, or
- a reasonable explanation as to why he was not selected for the team.

Of all the ingredients that combine to make a successful and happy team, none is more important than pride, pride in being selected, pride in representing a school or community or association, pride in doing the very best one can on every shift and in every practice, pride in physical condition, appearance, quality of performance. This type of pride can only be developed in a milieu where the coach has pride in what he is doing and in those young players who have been assigned to or selected by him. The proud athlete never looks for a "fall guy" to take the blame – he understands his own weakness or shortcoming; the proud athlete never needs excuses – for he understands that there are none; the proud athlete never questions the importance of practice, because he knows that only through practice will improvement occur; and the proud athelete never loses sight of the fact that sport is supposed to be fun.

A WORD ON THE
COACHING-TEACHING PROCESS

Many guiding principles have been developed by coaches and educators. A few are repeated here because of their appropriateness to hockey coaching:

(i)   Learning begins where the learner is, and not where the coach might hope him to be.

(ii)   Too much detail only confuses the learner; that is what is known as over-teaching or over-coaching.

(iii)   Not all players do things the same way; there is no one best way to perform, but there are ways that are better (more successful) than others.

(iv)   Repetition consolidates learning, provided the skill is repeated correctly.

(v)   Scrimmage encourages the practice of mistakes unless controlled.

(vi)   Activity of and by itself does not guarantee learning; understanding and meaningful activity are required.

(vii)   Players tend to practice skill strengths. Coaches must make sure that they eliminate the negative while they reinforce the positive.

(viii) Skills only become meaningful within the context of the game itself.

(ix)   Praise is a better educational force than blame.

Thus, the combination of good seasonal or unit and lesson or practice planning, sound coach-player, teacher-student, player-player and student-student communication, competent analysis and direction, and proper extrinsic motivation coupled with pride in performance and in leadership, should result in a situation that makes hockey the force for good, the sound educational medium, the fun that it was designed to be.

WHOLE SKILL VS. PART SKILL
TEACHING AND COACHING

Texts and manuals on athletic coaching often refer to the problems of over-teaching and under-teaching. These very real problems exist solely because teacher-coaches often forget the fact that athletes can only absorb specific amounts of skill instruction at any one time – no more – and, if boredom is to be avoided, no less! To fail to move them ahead skillwise is over-teaching in that too much time and attention is given to skills or parts of skills already mastered. To attempt to move them ahead too quickly is under-teaching in that they are not ready to absorb the skill challenges that complicated or involved patterns present.

The following example, in chart form, is used to illustrate the nature of the teaching-learning process. Let us assume that the coach is anxious to teach and have his players practice the complicated skill pattern of skating, headmanning the puck, receiving the pass back in a give and go situation, skating in on the goal, shooting, stopping and rebounding using the flip shot. The part skills involved are starting, gliding, passing, gliding, receiving the pass, speeding up, shooting, stopping and shooting again. At least five different patterns or sub-patterns may be used, depending on the ability level of each athlete:

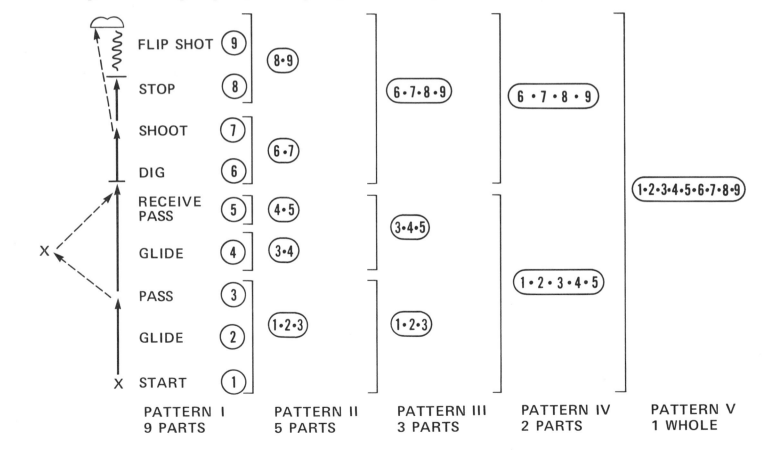

Pattern I includes 9 separate and distinct part-skills where each is taught and practiced as a separate entity.

Pattern II includes 5 sub-patterns, each the combination of two or more discrete skills.

Pattern III includes 3 sub-patterns while Pattern IV combines all 9 elements into but 2 sub-patterns.

Pattern V, the most complicated but most meaningful of the patterns, presents the 9 elements as a unity.

The lower the skill level of the performers, the more necessary it is to concentrate on Pattern V, breaking the skill down to smaller parts where absolutely necessary. The higher the skill level the more necessary it may become to "zero in" on one or more of the part skills for polishing and refining. Thus, it is conceivable that one or more players might best concentrate on giving and receiving passes (parts 3, 4 and 5 of Pattern I), while others who are quite adept at these skills work diligently on parts 7, 8 and 9 (shooting, stopping and rebounding), while still others work on the whole pattern (parts 1 to 9) until they develop an appreciation of the inter-relationship of the parts.

Good teaching/coaching requires the "individualization" of instruction and this, in turn, demands sound planning, expert diagnosis, high motivation and warm and reassuring communication.

6

Pre-Season Conditioning and Training

INTRODUCTION

It is commonplace to hear about football or basketball or baseball players who begin tossing the ball and running sprints and longer distances several weeks before the first formal practice is called; but little time and attention has been given to the matter of conditioning hockey players before the first ice session. This is particularly unfortunate for a number of reasons, including:

(a) the high cost of ice time which demands that every available minute be spent on hockey skills and patterns rather than on conditioning exercises that can equally well be done in another less expensive locale;

(b) the fact that hockey is a severe contact game that demands the ultimate in physical conditioning *before* the fact;

(c) the high incidence of early season injuries, many of which might have been prevented through proper exercise.

Therefore, it is suggested that every hockey coach and player address himself to the task of getting into "shape" for hockey before the first ice session.

HOW SOON TO BEGIN?

Since individuals vary so much in terms of strength, speed, endurance and cardio-respiratory adjustment to extreme work, the matter of establishing a starting date must be determined on an individual basis. Some may need to begin as early as eight weeks before the first ice session; others might reasonably wait until three weeks before they lace on their skates. The more active the young athlete has been during the vacation period, the less pre-season conditioning he will require. This is particularly true in those cases where a boy is involved actively in such desirable conditioning activities as soccer, cross country running, and weight training. By the same token, the youngster who has spent considerable time in swimming activities may require a greater amount of pre-season conditioning work because of the "softening" and "lengthening" effects of swimming on major muscles. A period of six weeks of training and conditioning may be considered as the "average" requirement and so the material presented in this section is based on this length of time. It can be added to or deleted from as circumstances demand.

HOW IMPORTANT IS PRE-SEASON CONDITIONING?

Three major reasons for pre-season conditioning have already been advanced in the first paragraph of this section. There are additional reasons, some of which are:

(a) the need for high conditioning to compensate for low or average skill;
(b) the fact that many games are won or lost in the third period when the fatigue factor is at its greatest;
(c) the improvement of learning rates by eliminating the deleterious factor of fatigue;
(d) the need for high levels of fitness in today's fore-checking type of game;
(e) the elimination or reduction of early season muscle soreness and discomfort.

ESTABLISHING CONDITIONING OBJECTIVES

Before embarking on a personal conditioning program, the players should establish a number of specific and attainable objectives. For example, a player may wish to:

(a) increase his wrist, hand and arm strength to improve his shot;
(b) develop a keen sense of puck control and awareness;
(c) increase the extent of his leg power or drive;
(d) train himself to persist without loss of performance quality for two or three minutes;
(e) reduce the time required to recover from violent exercise.

The nature of the objectives will dictate the content of the pre-season conditioning and training program.

It should be stressed here that very few individuals are so highly motivated that they will persist in a difficult (and sometimes boring) exercise program over a protracted period of time. Therefore, it is recommended that training and conditioning sessions be done in pairs or in small groups so that each assists in encouraging the others. Boys will resist quitting such a program when others are involved.

FOR ARMS, WRISTS AND HANDS

The following activities may prove interesting and useful:

(a) Stick wrestling with a partner
- see who can wrestle the stick from the other
- see who can make the stick turn in the other's hands

(b) Isometrics with hockey sticks
- simulating the forehand and backhand shot by placing the blade against a wall and pushing
- holding the stick firmly and resisting as a partner attempts to raise it

(c) Isometrics without equipment
- pushing hand against hand
- pushing a leg against a wall, hands on floor
- assuming a racer's crouch and pushing one foot against the wall
- pushing one hand against the side of the head
- etc.

(d) Weight training
- curls
- presses
- arm rotations
- etc.

(e) Shooting off a polished or waxed board against a wall or curtain

(f) Hand and arm wrestling contests with a partner

FOR LEG STRENGTH AND POWER

(a) Bicycling – and especially up moderate grades
(b) Cross country running – including some up-hill, level and down-hill running
(c) Soccer
(d) Circuit training – combining exercise work with running against time
(e) Jogging – and especially up stairs or grades
(f) Vertical jumping – emphasizing explosiveness
(g) Hopping on one foot, then the other, trying to maintain balance and at the same time, knock a partner off balance.

FOR PUCK CONTROL
AND AWARENESS

(a) Shooting off a polished or waxed board
(b) Stickhandling in place on a driveway, gym, basement floor
(c) Shooting against a wall and getting the rebounding puck under control
(d) Shooting at a net or practice board which has been appropriately marked
(e) Playing floor hockey at school, the Y or local recreation centre
(f) Increasing the distance of your shots – 20 feet, 30 feet, 40 feet, etc.
(g) Flipping shots into baskets or against marks on a wall

GETTING ACCUSTOMED
TO THE EQUIPMENT

There is probably no set of playing equipment that is more awkward or cumbersome than that used in hockey. As a result, many players feel extremely uncomfortable in their gear during the first week or so of a new season. It is recommended, therefore, that players:

(a) try on their equipment early to make sure that it fits properly;
(b) wear some of the equipment while performing pre-season exercises and drills, especially the gloves, helmet, shin pads and pants;
(c) try on their skates and boots to make sure they fit; lace up the boots to get used to the confined feeling.

All shooting drills should be performed with gloves on for only in this way will practical stick control develop.

SOME ADDITIONAL SUGGESTIONS

(a) Hockey makes heavy demands on the individual; adequate rest and good diet are essential ingredients to success.

(b) Foot care is essential; the skin should be toughened through the use of commercially available products designed for this purpose. Attention should be paid to the prevention of athlete's foot, ingrown toe nails, blisters.

(c) Stretching, abducting and adducting exercises are essential if early season groin injuries are to be reduced or avoided; the hurdling type exercise is particularly useful in this regard.

(d) In order to perform well and to avoid groin injury, skates must be properly sharpened. This should be done in advance of the first ice session.

(e) Goaltenders need pre-season conditioning as much as (or more than) defencemen and forwards. Running, stretching, falling, sliding, and stopping pucks are all useful activities in addition to the longer endurance type activities.

A SAMPLE SIX-WEEK PRE-SEASON CONDITIONING AND TRAINING PROGRAM

The following is typical of the many pre-season low-structured conditioning and training programs used by coaches in Canada and the United States:

FIFTH AND SIXTH WEEKS BEFORE THE FIRST ICE SESSION

- start running, easily at first, increase distance from half mile to two miles;
- start isometric exercises to build up arm, wrist and hand strength;
- include some up-hill running in the fifth week to develop good hockey posture.

THIRD AND FOURTH WEEKS BEFORE THE FIRST ICE SESSION

- continue with one to two mile runs;
- start some short sprints – 20 to 40 yards; repeat often;
- continue with isometrics; do six repetitions of each exercise three times each day;
- start your shooting (and goaltending) practice;
- start heavy exercise program: abdominals, legs, lower back, thighs;
- get out the hockey equipment and start checking it for fit and repair.

THE ROLE OF THE SCHOOL PHYSICAL EDUCATOR IN PRE-SEASON CONDITIONING

FIRST AND SECOND WEEKS BEFORE THE FIRST ICE SESSION

- do all exercises for speed;
- make sure the skates are ready for use;
- concentrate on dashes;
- increase your shooting and puckhandling drills;
- check the feet, begin toughening them up;
- work on wind through frequent demanding sprints.

FIRST ICE SESSION

- arrive early;
- make every second on the ice count;
- exhibit desire, interest, enthusiasm.

If it is not possible for the coach to organize and develop a pre-season conditioning program, then an approach should be made to the local high school or elementary school physical educator to promote such a program in class time, or before or after school, open to all who wish to get ready for school or community hockey leagues. In addition to the exercise sessions, he might be asked to promote inter-class soccer, floor hockey and/or cross country running for their own sake as well as for the pre-season training advantages to hockey candidates.

SOME SUGGESTIONS FOR THOSE FIRST FEW HOCKEY PRACTICES

It is not uncommon to find 60 or 80 or more boys arrive for the first hockey team try-out session. Since such a situation can lead only to anxiety and frustration on the part of the coach and the candidates, some specific suggestions may be in order:

(a) Call a meeting of all interested candidates well in advance of the first ice session. If the numbers are large, split the group into sections, making sure that a few of the returning players are included in each of the sections for comparison purposes.

(b) If possible, time this meeting so that information on pre-season conditioning programs and expectations can be passed along.

(c) Assign each candidate a number to be worn on the back of his jersey for identification purposes; otherwise, most will look the same – all in Montreal or Boston or Toronto sweaters, all or most wearing number 4 or number 9! Track or ski competitors' numbers are very useful for this purpose.

(d) Since cuts must be made early, and because skating and puckhandling ability are the key criteria in making initial cuts, concentrate early practice sessions on skating and puckhandling drills.

(e) Resist the temptation to devote all or most of the initial practice time to fatiguing conditioning drills. The net result will be an overly fatigued and low-motivated group which has real difficulty showing skill ability.

(f) If scrimmage is used liberally in early sessions to assist in the screening process, change the players ten at a time, regardless of position, emphasizing that you are mainly concerned about skating and puckhandling ability.

(g) Keep initial scrimmage shifts short, not more than two minutes and preferably about one and a half minutes; the rapid turn-over will add to the enthusiasm.

(h) If shooting practice is a part of early sessions, use both goals and, if more than two goaltenders are on hand, set up a third and, if needed, a fourth goal in the neutral zone beside the boards.

(i) Look for the very best skaters and puckhandlers, and the very poorest; they should stand out in the crowd. By so doing, the process of cutting is simplified.

(j) Give every candidate a fair opportunity to show what he can do; never cut boys at the end of the first work-out. This practice is humiliating and is hardly ever fair, at least in the eyes of the boys.

(k) When a candidate is cut from the roster, take the time to thank him for trying and make a suggestion or two as to what he might do to improve his chances in another season.

(l) Develop and keep up to date a roster list so that the boys know where they stand.

GOALERS	DEFENCEMEN	LEFT WINGS	CENTERS	RIGHT WINGS
1. _____	1. _____	1. _____	1. _____	1. _____
2. _____	2. _____	2. _____	2. _____	2. _____
3. _____	3. _____	3. _____	3. _____	3. _____
4. _____	4. _____	4. _____	4. _____	4. _____
	5. _____	5. _____	5. _____	5. _____
	6. _____	6. _____	6. _____	6. _____
	7. _____			
	8. _____			

It is obvious that a coach cannot retain the services of thirty players but such a list will allow each player to understand his present position and to work harder to retain his spot or to move up the list. Many players cut themselves either because they know they can't make it or because they have not had any encouragement from the coach. A roster list is a form of communication and talent evaluation and is useful particularly when changes are made every other day based on performance in practice.

Finally, in these early practice sessions, make sure that the boys know what you want them to do *before* they step on the ice and make sure they understand that no time can be wasted in adjusting equipment, tightening skate laces, changing helmets or other equipment. Failure to be ready to go is an indicator of attitude, and a good attitude is the first step on the path to the achievement of pride (cf. Part V).

WARM-UP ACTIVITIES

It is essential that the coach develop an interesting and meaningful warm-up phase for each hockey class or practice, one that can be done with little wasted time and, after the first session or two, few verbal explanations. If the players *understand* that it is to their advantage to be properly warmed-up then little difficulty should be experienced in having them take this phase seriously.

A large number of on-ice exercises and activities have been developed down through the years. The following is only a sample program; additions or substitutions of activities may be appropriate.

1. As soon as the players step on the ice, they should complete two or three laps of the rink at medium speed, emphasizing the length of stride and the coordination of legs and shoulder-arm action.

2. The next few laps (or half laps if another team is sharing the ice) should include:

    (a) stretching upwards and backwards, stick in both hands, then downwards pressing the stick against the front of the ankles;

(b) holding the stick in both hands in front of the body and at shoulder level and then attempting to kick the stick with each leg; then raising each leg alternately and pressing upwards with the stick.

(c) lengthening the stride to the point that the forward leg is bent, the trailing leg is stretched out behind with the inside of the blade dragging on the ice, and alternating legs.

3. Players should now take positions on the corner or center ice face-off circles and skate clockwise then counter-clockwise, emphasizing the step-over, stick on the ice, low foot recovery.

4. Since speed is of the essence in hockey, one or two laps (three or four half laps) should now be skated at full speed.

5. Finally, players should assist in warming-up the goaltenders through shooting practice emphasizing keeping the shots low and on target.

Where two teams are sharing the ice and each has two goaltenders, it is important to warm-up all goaltenders. Thus, one should occupy the goal, the second should take a position against the end boards and near a corner. Half the players can work on one goaler while the other half assist the second.

This sample warm-up can be completed in about five minutes plus shooting time and, from the standpoint of injury prevention, can be considered absolutely essential. It should be stated here that it is *not* the purpose of a warm-up to condition, overload or fatigue the players; rather it is designed to elevate body temperature, loosen up the muscles, and put the players in a proper frame of mind for more taxing activity. A warm-up which fatigues the players does nothing more than reduce the attention span and inhibit the learning rate.

A FINAL WORD

Unfortunately, few coaches have adequate ice time at their disposal. In these instances use should be made of the classroom and gymnasium or recreation room for supplementary practice sessions. A great deal of conditioning work can be accomplished in this way; continuity from day to day can be established; ice drills can be rehearsed; the fun element can be emphasized through the use of inter-squad soccer, floor hockey or conditioning competitions (cf. Part V, B).

7

Fifteen Questions
Coaches Most Often Ask

INTRODUCTION

On the basis of my coaching clinic experience, it is obvious that a number of rather common questions continue to bother many of our amateur coaches and their players. Time and again the same questions, framed in slightly different ways, are raised; far too often the questions remain unresolved, at least in the minds of those attending the clinics.

The following are but fifteen of the many questions which students of hockey – coaches and participants – have asked the writer in recent years. The answers are, of necessity, rather brief, but the important underlying principles have been emphasized in the hope that these answers may have wider application.

A. QUESTIONS RE ORGANIZATION, PHILOSOPHY, ADMINISTRATION

Question No. 1

HOCKEY PROTECTIVE EQUIPMENT IS VERY EXPENSIVE. HOW IMPORTANT IS IT FOR THE YOUNG PLAYER TO BE FULLY EQUIPPED?

Answer:

The younger the player the more susceptible he is to injury, simply because of his lack of skill development. Hockey demands a well-refined sense of balance, considerable stamina and strength, and a high degree of flexibility and agility. For these reasons then, and because we must do all in our power to protect our charges from injury, it is suggested that all hockey players wear full sets of protective equipment. This set should include:

(a) a good helmet, properly adjusted, with excellent coverage of the back of the head and the temples, and fastened with a strong chin strap;

(b) properly-fitted shoulder pads that protect the point of the shoulders and the collarbones;

(c) elbow pads that adequately protect the elbow from falls and dasher bumps;

(d) mouth or tooth protectors that are worn internally or over the mouth;

(e) shin pads that cover the shin, the sides of the lower legs, the knee, and the area above the knee and below the thigh pads;

(f) gloves that properly protect the fingers, top of the thumb, the wrist, both front and back, and part of the lower arm;

(g) athletic supporter plus a separate cup-supporter for full protection of the genitals;

(h) hockey pants that include good protective elements for the base of the spine, the lower ribs, lower back and the thighs (note: this must be the most poorly designed piece of hockey protective equipment and one worthy of considerable study and experimentation);

(i) the best possible skates and boots that the player can afford, bearing in mind that the three most important parts of these items are: the counters (the area which supports the heels), the blades (a good quality steel is required here), and the toe caps (designed to protect the toes from blows).

Some players like to wear ankle protectors and these are recommended. Goalers should exercise care in selecting their boots and their face-masks. The total cost of equipping a hockey player is high; but the chances of injury when ill-protected or under-protected are also high. Thus, costs have to be assessed in human terms. The three major expense items are the pants, skates and boots, and gloves; the rest of the items can be purchased in a wide variety of price ranges.

Question No. 2

FIGHTING SEEMS TO HAVE BECOME AN INTEGRAL PART OF HOCKEY. HOW FAR SHOULD COACHES AND PLAYERS GO TO ELIMINATE THIS ELEMENT FROM THE GAME?

Answer:

Because hockey is a body-contact sport and because it is played at a very high speed, there is an almost natural tendency on occasion to see tempers flare in proportion to the amount of contact and speed. Fighting should *not* be encouraged; that is not the name of the game; but brawling must be eliminated. The National Hockey League in 1971-72 introduced a new rule which has done wonders in terms of eliminating bench-emptying and mass brawling from hockey. When a fight erupts, any third or subsequent player who becomes involved is ejected from the game. In my view, all amateur hockey should follow suit. Young players will react in tense situations consistent with the behaviour of their coaches. If coaches can maintain their "cool", and if coaches, in so doing, insist that fights be restricted to the two original combatants, then I think we will have done all that can and must be done to retain the best elements of the world's fastest game.

Question No. 3

WHAT SHOULD THE COACH'S ROLE BE IN TERMS OF ADMINISTERING EMERGENCY FIRST AID?

Answer:

Because very few of our amateur teams can afford the services of a qualified trainer, most coaches are required to wear a number of hats, including that of "on-the-spot" trainer. In my view, the coach can carry out these responsibilities quite adequately if he bears but a few basic principles in mind:

(a) in instances where severe cuts are suffered, apply direct pressure on the wound.—use a towel, bandage, gauze, or what-have-you. Get the player to the doctor as soon as possible for stitching.

(b) in instances where a break, sprain or strain is suffered, follow the I-C-E formula, i.e., Ice, Compression, Elevation. A cold pack is an essential part of the coach-trainer's equipment; elastic bandages are handy things to have around for compression purposes. If the break-sprain-strain is in the ankle, *leave the boot on*—it is the perfect compression bandage. All such injuries should be X-rayed so follow-up is very important here.

(c) in instances where unconsciousness results from a fall or collision, it should be assumed that the injury is serious and therefore requires immediate medical attention. Do *not* get the player back on his feet—nature has assisted recovery by dropping him to a lying position. Such ridiculous practices as leg-pumping should be avoided; they can often aggravate the injury.

In all instances record the nature, time and locale of the injury as well as the steps you took in dealing with it. This information will come in handy at a later date if and when insurance claims are filed. Finally, because most coaches are not medical doctors and because medical doctors have been trained to handle major injuries, the decision regarding the player's return to action should rest with the doctor. Respect his judgment in this regard; it is one way in which you can show that you place the welfare of the player above the results of a game.

Question No. 4

IT HAS BEEN SUGGESTED TIME AND AGAIN THAT HOCKEY AND EDUCATION ARE INCOMPATIBLE. DO YOU AGREE?

Answer:

Not at all! For many years it was assumed that the *only* path to the National Hockey League was the Junior "A" series in Western Canada or Ontario. But dozens of players have made the jump to the major leagues via the college, national team or senior routes. In addition, a number of players have combined Junior "A" play with education and carried both off extremely well. As this is being written no less than fifty-four college graduates or former college hockey players are participating in the N.H.L.! It should be stated that it took the schools and colleges a long time to develop the sort of hockey programs that were truly developmental. And many still have a long way to go in this regard. But college coaching has improved, schedules have been augmented, rinks have become available, seasons have been lengthened, practice time has been increased. There still exists a real need for amateur operators to adjust their schedules, trips and play-offs to the school academic calendar; in far too many instances conflicts do exist between games and examinations. But here again real progress is being made. Interestingly enough, a 1967 study in Ontario showed that Junior hockey players do *not* drop out of school; they tend to remain until graduation though graduation may be impeded by as much as a year. Thus, if superb performers like Tony Esposito, Red Berenson, Keith Magnussen, Ken Dryden, Carl Brewer, Eric Nesterenko, Bill MacMillan, Red Hay, and so many others could combine hockey and education, others should be able to follow suit. The key to the problem is a proper articulation between the hockey year and the school year. And here is where school people can exert real influence and leadership.

Question No. 5

A LARGE NUMBER OF SUMMER HOCKEY SCHOOLS ARE NOW AVAILABLE TO YOUNG PLAYERS. ARE THESE WORTHWHILE? HOW DOES ONE SELECT A PARTICULARLY GOOD ONE?

Answer:

The growth of summer hockey schools has been one of the truly amazing phenomena of the past few years. Some operators are even now in the business of selling franchises! A review of the hockey school advertisements in any of the major hockey publications will show just how wide the choice is. I think one should bear in mind the fact that hockey schools grew in number and popularity as summer camps of the tripping variety decreased either in number or popularity or increased in cost beyond the ability of thousands of boys. In addition there is something very attractive about playing hockey out-of-season; it is a bit of a novelty; there is also something very appealing about being able to rub shoulders with hockey idols. I believe you can pick a good hockey school on these bases:

(a) the amount of ice time per boy per day;
(b) the number of boys on the ice at any one time;
(c) the amount of repeat "business" the school gets;
(d) the length of time each instructor is required to remain at the school (some "name" players only lend their names to schools; others appear for the opening and closing only; others remain on the job for an extended period of time);
(e) the balance of the staff (ideally, each staff should include name players, younger players, coaches or other administrative personnel, trainers, and a sprinkling of professional educators);
(f) the reactions of players and their parents to a school previously attended (many schools will provide you with a list of those from your area who have attended in the past).

Hockey school should be *fun*, after all, it is part of the boy's summer vacation. But it should also increase his skill level in the basics (skating and puckhandling particularly) and his understanding and appreciation of the game itself. It should take into account the age level of the participants and should provide the sort of off-ice leadership and counselling that are so important in this type of operation. Finally, *good* schools should be encouraged; *bad* schools should be reported and, hopefully, eliminated.

Question No. 6

THERE IS A GREAT DEAL OF PRESSURE IN OUR AREA TO ORGANIZE HOCKEY LEAGUES FOR YOUNGSTERS OF 6, 7 AND 8 YEARS OF AGE. HOW YOUNG SHOULD WE START?

Answer:

Youngsters should begin to skate almost as soon as they can safely walk and run. Skating is a fairly natural skill in that it involves the out-turning of the feet, arm opposition, straight back, and so forth. In my view, however, once you place a hockey stick in the hands of poor skaters you almost immediately impede their skating skill development. They start to lean on the stick, to count on it for support, to allow the stick to throw them off balance. Thus, when a boy can skate reasonably well, the time has arrived to show him how to carry a stick. At this point the game should be *modified*. For example, many of the youngest players

can get all the fun they need by playing across the ice, and a number of games can be held at the same time. Again, the icing rule presumes that players know how to pass and receive a pass. Our youngest performers don't! So the rule should not be applied. Youngsters will tend to follow the puck like so many bees after honey. This is bad hockey but it is good fun. Just so long as they are skating, controlling their sticks, and having fun, then hockey is fine for them. The tendency has been to over-structure, over-teach, over-regiment, and thus over-kill enthusiasm. In my experience I have found that pee-wee organized hockey is as low as we should go! (A pee-wee is a youngster in the age 10-11 group). If an exceptional 8 or 9 year old should happen on the scene, then he is probably ready to compete with 10 and 11 year olds at the pee-wee level. Those who support highly structured hockey for children in the 6, 7 and 8 year old group may be well motivated, but I doubt that the children are as enthusiastic as their adult organizers.

Question No. 7

THE PRESSURE TO WIN, PARTICULARLY WITH RESPECT TO OUR YOUNGEST TEAMS, FORCES ME TO USE THE SAME FEW PLAYERS FOR MOST OF THE GAME. THUS, MANY YOUNGSTERS ARE NOT GETTING THEIR SHARE OF ICE TIME. HOW CAN ONE LICK THIS PROBLEM?

Answer:

The answer to this question can really be found in one's philosophy with respect to hockey competition for young children. In more highly organized hockey – Bantam, Midget, Juvenile, High School, Junior, and so forth, it is sound coaching to get the maximum mileage from your best players. Coaches usually begin and end each period with their top line; in addition, these players often form part of the power play unit; occasionally, one or two of them might also be used to "kill" penalties. *But*, when we are involved in hockey programs with very young players, I think it is important that coaches agree to make complete changes every 2 to 2½ minutes. In a large number of instances, players are set up in groups of five – three forwards and two defencemen. The most skilled group on Team "A" is always matched with the most skilled group on Team "B", and so on down the line. One official is assigned the responsibility of timing shifts. When the 2 or 2½ minute mark is reached, the whistle is blown and a complete change is made. In this way every player gets equal ice time. The system will require some interpretation to parents who cause most of our "pressure" problems. In many hockey leaders' views, the principle is important enough to insist upon even to the point of putting one's coaching assignment (usually voluntary) on the line!

B. QUESTIONS OF A TECHNICAL NATURE

Question No. 8

VERY OFTEN WE ARE FORCED TO MAKE SUBSTITUTIONS WHILE THE PLAY CONTINUES. HOW CAN THESE CHANGES BE EFFECTIVELY MADE?

Answer:

There are a couple of important principles here:

(a) You have to establish a routine on your players' bench – players should be instructed to leave the ice via one gate and to enter the ice through the other gate (if one exists) or by scrambling over the boards.

(b) One individual – the spare goaltender, the extra forward, the fifth defenceman, the manager or even the coach should be responsible for opening the gate so that players can get off the ice quickly.

(c) As soon as a change is made, the coach should indicate the people who will be involved in the next change so that they are ready to move if a change-on-the-fly is necessary.

(d) When a change is to be made the players involved on the bench should stand up so that their counterparts on the ice can see them.

(e) When scrambling over the boards, the stick should precede the player so that there is no possibility of injuring a teammate in one's haste to join the play.

(f) Changes-on-the-fly should only be made when the puck is on its way to the opposition's end of the ice or when the puck is in possession of a teammate who can, without causing an icing whistle, shoot the puck the length of the ice or, without causing an off-side, feed the puck to a player entering the game from the bench.

This process requires frequent practice; efficiency will not be easily attained. But if your players understand what you are trying to do and how you insist on doing it, then real expertise can be achieved.

Question No. 9

WHAT SYSTEM SHOULD A COACH ADOPT TO PROTECT A ONE-GOAL LEAD WITH BUT A FEW MINUTES TO PLAY?

Answer:

There are probably as many different answers to this question as there are coaches. Some suggest that you have your players fall back and protect their defensive zone, sometimes referred to as the "kitty-bar-the-door" system; others feel that an aggressive forechecking game is the answer, based on the premise that you should not let the opposition get organized; still others suggest that you should put your best checkers on the ice and stick to a close checking, back-checking oriented type of game. A fourth alternative often suggested is that you place your best puck-control players on the ice and attempt to control the game

yourselves. There are advantages and disadvantages to all four systems, and to the others that are used from time to time. Your decision will probably be based on the quality of your personnel: if you have good solid goaltending, you may wish to play a defensive game at your blue line; if you have excellent forecheckers but only mediocre puckhandlers, you may wish to adopt a forechecking system. Regardless of the system advocated, possession is still nine-tenths of winning, so try to get the puck, and keep it!

Question No. 10

ARE THERE ANY RULES-OF-THUMB WHICH SHOULD BE APPLIED IN PUTTING TOGETHER A FORWARD LINE?

Answer:

The way coaches are switching players around these days, one would think not! But, in point of fact, there are two guiding principles which are usually applied although not necessarily in an either-or-way.

(a) Find your *best three* forwards and set them up as a line; hopefully, they will be your goal producers and will be sufficiently talented that they can overcome the checking line sent out against them, or

(b) Find your *best two* forwards and set them up as two-thirds of a line, then assign a checker to the line to provide balance and to allow the top two scorers to concentrate more on offence and less (though only slightly less) on checking.

150

When you have established your first line, then repeat the process for the second line, that is, select your next best three forwards or next best two forwards and a checker. Setting up a third line is always a problem; assuming that your talent is limited, I would think you would want to retain the services of your best skaters and checkers for that third line. You probably will not be able to expect too much in the way of goal production from them, but you may reasonably expect them to prevent the opposition from scoring more than one or two goals against them in any one game.

It is interesting to look at a few of the top professional lines:

Howe-Lindsay-Abel of Detroit fame – a superb play-maker in Abel, a prolific scorer in Howe, a better-than-average scorer and checker in Lindsay. All three of them are mentioned when experts try to assemble an all-time, all-star team. Obviously, Detroit put their three best together.

Blake-Richard-Lach of the Canadiens – the honest worker and backchecker (Blake), the fancy play-maker (Lach), the prolific scorer (Richard) – two offensive players and a superb defensive player who developed into a tremendous offensive threat.

Esposito-Cashman-Hodge of Boston – the greatest goal-scorer of them all in any one season in Esposito, the strong skater, checker, play-maker in Hodge, and the tireless checker and position player in Cashman.

Mahovlich-Mahovlich-Lafleur of the Canadiens – a line composed of a high scoring rookie (Lafleur) whose checking leaves much to be desired, and two big, strong, two-way hockey players in the Mahovlich brothers who also serve as penalty-killers and power play attackers.

Sanderson-Walton-Westfall of Boston – a checker combined with a checker combined with a checker. Because of their checking ability, they also get their fair share of goals.

Perhaps the most conventional line in professional hockey today is the Toronto combination of Ellis (checker and accurate shooter from the blue line), Henderson (prolific scorer), and the very heady perpetual motion play-maker, Norm Ullman.

Thus, a number of obvious conclusions can be reached: lines may be composed of two or more "big guns", two or three checkers, or one prolific scorer, one play-maker and one checker. The choice is really a matter of individual preference, and what brings success!

Question No. 11

OUR PLAYERS USE THE SLAP SHOT ALMOST EXCLUSIVELY. AS A RESULT, THEIR ACCURACY QUOTIENT IS LOW. WHAT MIGHT I DO TO REDUCE THIS PROBLEM?

Answer:

It must be admitted at the outset that the slap shot is the easiest of the four or five different types of shots to deliver. Lack of strength is compensated for by the speed of the delivery; curved sticks add considerably to the ease of execution; so many of the professionals use it that younger players are bound to copy them. I would like to think that a boy might become convinced of its relative ineffectiveness (assuming that it is, of course) by keeping a shooting chart on himself and his team-mates. Place an X on a chart at the point at which shots are delivered; if the shot misses the goal entirely or if the shot is "flubbed", then circle the X. Then work out a shooting accuracy figure for each player. If a boy takes, let us say, 6 shots on goal during a game or scrimmage, none score, only 1 is on the goal, and the remaining five are off target, then his scoring average is 0 and his accuracy average is 17%. Do likewise during shooting practice; if his average remains low, then suggest that he try using the snap or wrist shot in the next practice. Compare the statistics and that may be enough to convince him that he just won't score unless he improves his consistency and accuracy.

Question No. 12

A NUMBER OF TEAMS ALWAYS SEEM TO TRY TO CARRY THE PUCK INTO THE ATTACK-ING ZONE WHILE OTHERS VERY OFTEN OR INVARIABLY SHOOT THE PUCK IN FROM THE NEUTRAL ZONE. ARE THERE ANY RULES-OF-THUMB THAT MIGHT BE APPLIED?

Answer:

Obviously, once you achieve possession of the puck you want to retain it. If you do, the opposition can't score on you and your chances of scoring are increased. So the first general rule is to retain possession whenever you can. There are, however, at least four situations when it may be desirable to shoot the puck into the attacking zone from the neutral zone:

(a) when you are changing personnel on-the-fly;
(b) when one or two wings are breaking fast towards the opposition's blue line, they seem to have the "jump" on the defenders because of their speed and are almost certain of regaining possession of the puck if it is shot in;
(c) when there is a danger that one or more wings may skate in to the defensive zone off-side;
(d) when the defending defencemen are playing in the neutral zone just outside their blue line and the attacking wings are covered by backcheckers, thus eliminating any possibility of a passing play.

It is absolutely imperative that you practice the timing of this manoeuvre; it is also essential that your wings be quite expert at forechecking in the event that a defender gets to the puck first. The options that might be employed when you regain possession have been outlined in the section on offensive hockey in this manual.

Question No. 13

HOW MIGHT A COACH MAINTAIN THE INTEREST OF HIS PLAYERS IN A LOSING SEASON?

Answer:

This is always a difficult problem, particularly with amateurs. At the risk of sounding trite, the coach's main task in this regard is to put everything into proper perspective. Youngsters should take stock of themselves and their chances for success at the beginning of the season. If the prospects are dim, then alternatives to winning have to be found. A few examples might be:

(a) ratio of goals for and against – can we improve it this year?
(b) shots on goal in each game – can we increase ours and reduce theirs from game to game?
(c) goals scored by them on rebounds – can we reduce or eliminate these?
(d) individual player improvement – how many successful passes? shooting accuracy? speed improvement? checking consistency? etc.

In short, a coach can reduce the game to a number of sub-games, each with a specific objective, each with an evaluative, self-testing yardstick. Surprisingly, as young players begin to dwell less on the final outcome and more on self-improvement, the team will begin to win its share of games. I suppose that I'm really saying that the coach should accentuate the positive and stop his charges from putting all of their eggs in the basket of games-won.

Question No. 14

WHY IS IT THAT SO MANY CLINIC INSTRUCTORS MINIMIZE THE IMPORTANCE OF SCRIMMAGE IN PRACTICES?

Answer:

There is so much to learn in hockey that, as a starting point, the coach must plan and use every available minute to advantage. When a team begins to scrimmage, there is a tendency to emphasize expediency over correct performance, and to coast or move at three-quarter speed, particularly if you have only three lines available. Thus, many scrimmages tend to encourage players to practice and reinforce bad habits, sloppy performance. But scrimmage is a good motivator, and should be used when a needed boost in enthusiasm is required. Going one step further, line rushes, plays coming out of the defensive zone, power plays, playing short-handed or with advantage, are all legitimate drills; they are also isolated game patterns that combine specific practice with contact, competition and self-evaluation. A well-structured practice that includes parts of the game done over and over again at full speed can be a thoroughly enjoyable and motivating experience. From a diagnostic standpoint, it is much easier to coach when you are directing your attention to *one* phase of the game rather than to the game in its entirety.

153

Question No. 15

WE HEAR A GREAT DEAL ABOUT THE
QUALITY OF EUROPEAN HOCKEY. ARE THERE
THINGS WE CAN LEARN FROM THE RUSSIANS,
THE SWEDES, AND SO FORTH, TO IMPROVE
OUR NORTH AMERICAN GAME?

Answer:

Unquestionably, yes! The Europeans stress five
things that have received only short shrift in Canada
and the United States:

(a) *superb* pre-season physical conditioning, particularly in the area of strength development;
(b) meticulous passing and receiving – they spend
hundreds of hours perfecting their deliveries and
receptions;

(c) highly refined position play – each player understands that certain positions must always be
filled (cf. Part II, Offensive Team Play);
(d) a great emphasis on team work – as opposed to the
individual or star system that has dominated our
hockey;
(e) the development of progressively more challenging
self-testing drills.

It should be added that they have not developed as
yet our expertise in individual skill performance; they
still have quite a way to go to match our best in
checking; and their goaltending is far inferior to what
we have become used to expecting. A happy combination of the North American style of play and the
European physical conditioning and mastery of passing
may make for a better game for all parts of the world.

Appendix

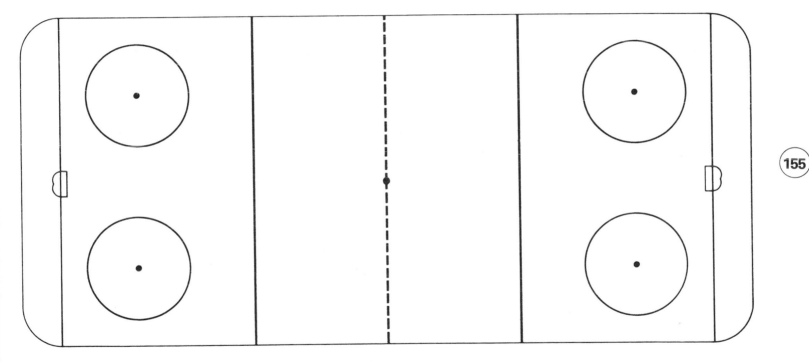

DRILL SHEET

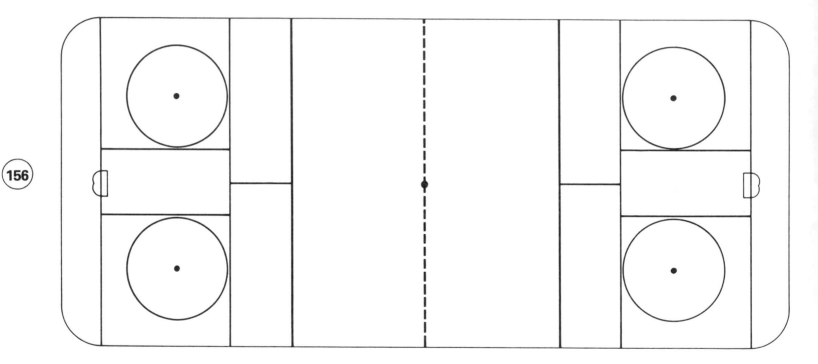

GOALTENDING CHART

PRACTICE PLAN FORM

TEAM _____ PRACTICE NO. _____ DATE _____	TIME
1. Warm-up –	——
2. Skating – passing – puckhandling –	——
3. Special area No. 1 –	——
4. Shooting – goaltending –	——
5. Special area No. 2 –	——
6. Controlled scrimmage –	——
7. Conditioning –	——
Individual instruction with:	
Comments –	

Suggested Readings

It was indicated in the Introduction that many texts have been written on hockey in recent years. The following are a few which are recommended to coaches and players who wish to learn more about the many facets of the game covered in this text and the many, many more which time and space prevented me from including.

For suggestions on teaching the youngest children to skate –

Larivière, G., and Bournival, J.: *Hockey, The Right Start* (Toronto: Holt, Rinehart and Winston, 1969).

For an exciting new approach to the art of power skating –

Wild, John: *Power Skating* (Scarborough, Ontario: Prentice-Hall, 1971).

For some excellent tips on goaltending and defensive hockey –

Patrick, L., and Monahan, L.: *Let's Play Hockey* (Toronto: Macmillan, 1957).

For excellent suggestions on conditioning, training, and skill development –

Percival, L.: *The Hockey Handbook* (Toronto: Copp, Clark, 1951).

For some marvellous tips on stickhandling, passing, and shooting –

Bathgate, A., and Wolff, B.: *Andy Bathgate's Hockey Secrets* (Englewood Cliffs, N. J.: Prentice-Hall, 1963).

Two "hand-outs" for the younger players –

Hockey Handbook (Toronto: Harris-Keon Hockey School, 1971).
Tips on Power Hockey (Toronto: C.C.M., 1970).

A little pamphlet that is worth its weight in gold –

Helpful Hints for Hockey Coaches (Toronto: Crown Life Insurance).

ABOUT THE AUTHOR

John Meagher is a native Montrealer who received his early education and hockey experience at Loyola High School, – one of the truly great sports-oriented secondary schools in Canada. He holds a Bachelor of Arts degree from Loyola College, a Bachelor of Science degree in Physical Education from McGill University and both the Master of Science and Doctor of Education degrees from The Pennsylvania State University.

His career as a player included four years of minor hockey, three years of high school hockey, six years of college and university hockey at Loyola and McGill and one year of Junior "A" hockey with the Montreal Royals.

His coaching career included positions at Westmount High School in Montreal, Macdonald College, and with the McGill University Indians.

Since moving to New Brunswick in 1957 to establish the first School of Physical Education in the Atlantic Region, he has served as a member of the Canadian National Study Committee on Hockey, instructor at four Regional Hockey Institutes, lecturer at the first National Coaching School sponsored by the Canadian Amateur Hockey Association, and as a member of the teaching staff at the St. Andrews Summer Hockey School, – one of the largest and most prestigious schools of its kind in North America.

In 1971 he was commissioned by the Canadian Government to prepare two major in-depth studies on possible reorganization of amateur hockey in Canada.

This text was prepared on the basis of these experiences and as a logical follow-up to the dozens of undergraduate, extension and workshop courses in hockey he has offered in Eastern Canada and the United States over the past twenty years.